Funky Knits

Knitting know-how for hip young things

Carol Meldrum and Julie Marchington

INTERWEAVE PRESS

A QUARTO BOOK

Copyright © 2006 Quarto Inc.

INTERWEAVE PRESS

Published in North America by
Interweave Press LLC
201 East Fourth Street
Loveland, CO 80537-5655
www.interweave.com
All rights reserved.

Conceived, designed,
and produced by
Quarto Publishing plc
The Old Brewery
6 Blundell Street
London N7 9BH

QUA: FKN

Project editor: Michelle Pickering
Editors: Eva Yates, Jean Lampe
Art editor: Anna Knight
Designer: Lizzie Ballantyne
Assistant art director: Penny Cobb
Photographer: Martin Norris
Models: Unity Blundell, Sam Phillips,
Trisha Telep
Illustrator: Kuo Kang Chen

Art director: Moira Clinch
Publisher: Paul Carslake

Color separation by
Provision Pte Ltd, Singapore
Printed by Star Standard
Pte Ltd, Singapore

Library of Congress Cataloging-
in-Publication Data
Meldrum, Carol.
  Funky knits : knitting know-how
for hip young things / Carol
Meldrum and Julie Marchington,
authors.
       p. cm.
  Includes index.
  ISBN 1-59668-003-2
  1. Knitting--Patterns.
I. Marchington, Julie. II. Title.
  TT825.M44 2006
  746.43'2--dc22
              2005027196

10 9 8 7 6 5 4 3 2 1

Contents

Chapter 3:
Night Owls

Chapter 5:
Punk Garage Rocks

Chapter 4:
Home Comforts

Chapter 6:
Festival Folk

Introduction

Knitting is back—it's fun, it's fashionable, and it's funky! Knitting is a great excuse for getting together with like-minded friends and a fun way of making new ones. The knitting circles of old have been replaced and revamped with groups of knitters getting together wherever the vibe takes them—you can now spot knitters in cafes, in the park, on the bus, and even in wine bars.

This book is a celebration of the growing urban knitting movement that is happening throughout the world. It is aimed at creative people, male and female, who want to make gorgeous garments and accessories that are fun to knit and funky to wear, and who want to express their personality and their lifestyle through the medium of knitting.

The first chapter explains all the knitty gritty—the key skills and techniques that you will need—with step-by-step illustrations so that even complete novices can get started. The rest of the book is project-based, with each chapter of projects designed to reflect a range of different knitting personalities and moods, so you are guaranteed to find a project that will make you itch to stitch. Dip into the themed chapters and you are sure to find something to suit your own knitting

personality,
whether you are
a domestic goddess, a decadent
glamour puss, a skater girl or
boy, a hippy chick, or a groovy guy.
Inspired by modern city life, more
than 30 original designs for clothing,
accessories, gifts, and homewares are
featured, demonstrating what an accessible,
multifunctional, and flexible
craft this is.
The purpose of the book is
to show you exactly how much fun
knitting can be—it's no longer
something that only your granny
does! You can follow the project
instructions exactly, but don't
be afraid to experiment and
develop your own style, and
remember that knitting is a
sociable activity that can be
done anytime, anyplace,
anywhere. So, stop
twiddling your thumbs
and pick up your
needles—knitting
is the perfect
chill-out
activity.

chapter 1

THE KNITTY GRITTY

The great thing about knitting is that the materials, equipment, and skills you need to get started are pretty basic—some yarn and needles, and a couple of stitch techniques. That's it! If you're a complete novice, you can learn everything you need to know to make the projects in this chapter. If you already know how to knit, use this chapter as a resource to refresh your skills whenever you need to.

Materials

The only essential material you need to make the projects in this book is yarn. Although the specific yarns used to make the projects are listed on pages 126–127, you may wish to knit a project using a different yarn. Understanding the qualities of the various types of yarn available will help you choose one that is suitable.

Linen

Silk

Cotton

Wool

Yarns and weights

Yarn is made by spinning fibers of material together. Yarn fibers can be split into two categories: natural and synthetic. The naturals are animal fibers, such as wool, alpaca, and cashmere, and vegetable fibers, such as cotton, hemp, and linen. Synthetic fibers are made from a range of substances but all are manmade. Some yarns are a blend of natural and synthetic.

Each strand of fiber used to make yarn is called a ply, and different types of yarn are made from different numbers of plies. The type of fiber, number of plies, and method of spinning all affect the thickness and weight of the finished yarn. Yarn weights vary from very fine to very thick. Traditionally, there were standard thicknesses of yarn, such as worsted and bulky, but nowadays there are so many different blends and fancy yarns available that these terms may be used for different weights of yarn from one yarn spinner to another. The best thing to do if you are unsure of the weight is to check the ball band to see what size needle to use (see page 11).

Viscose/polyester

The following weights of yarn have been used in this book:

- **Fingering weight:** Fine yarn usually knitted on size 1–3 (2.25–3.25 mm) needles.
- **Sportweight:** About one-and-a-half times the thickness of fingering-weight yarn, usually knitted on size 3–5 (3.25–3.75 mm) needles.
- **DK (double knitting):** Just under twice the thickness of fingering-weight yarn, usually knitted on size 5–7 (3.75–4.5 mm) needles.
- **Aran:** Just under twice the thickness of double-knitting yarn, usually knitted on size 7–9 (4.5–5.5 mm) needles.
- **Bulky/super bulky:** This covers a wide variety of weights, knitted on size 10 (6 mm) needles upward.

Ball bands

Whether it comes in ball or hank form, the yarn you buy will have a band around it that lists lots of important information.

Weight and length: This gives the weight of the ball in ounces or grams and the length of the yarn in yards or meters. This information is useful for calculating the total length needed to complete a project. You can then compare alternative yarns to see whether more or fewer balls are needed to match the required length.

Washing instructions: These tell you how to wash and take care of the yarn once knitted.

Gauge: This is the standard number of stitches and rows measured over 4" (10 cm) using the recommended needle size and stockinette stitch. However, check the pattern because the designer may have something else in mind.

Shade and dye lot numbers: The shade number is the manufacturer's reference to a particular color; the dye lot number refers to a specific batch of yarn dyed in that color at the same time. The lot number will change from batch to batch. When knitting a project, it is important to buy sufficient yarn from the same dye lot because these can vary slightly in color. If you are not certain how many balls you will need, it is always best to buy one extra.

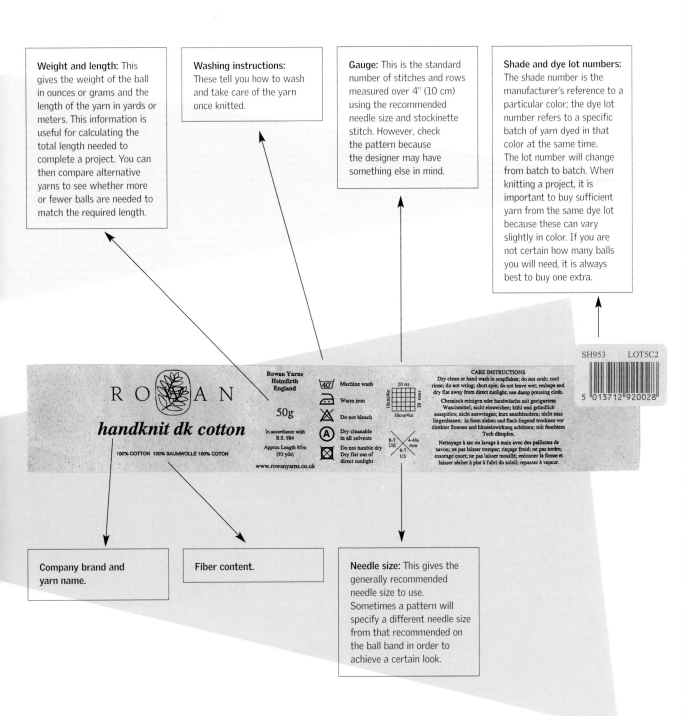

Company brand and yarn name.

Fiber content.

Needle size: This gives the generally recommended needle size to use. Sometimes a pattern will specify a different needle size from that recommended on the ball band in order to achieve a certain look.

Substituting yarns

The specific yarns used to knit the patterns in this book are listed on pages 126–127, but you can substitute an alternative yarn if you prefer, or if you cannot find the exact yarn used. However, there are a number of things that you need to check before purchasing a substitute yarn and casting on.

1 Calculate the total length of yarn needed to complete the project by multiplying the number of balls by the length of yarn per ball (you will find this information at the beginning of each project).

2 Then divide the total length of yarn required by the length per ball of the substitute yarn. This will give the number of substitute balls required.

3 Check that the manufacturer's recommended needle size for the actual yarn used matches the recommended needle size for the substitute yarn. This will ensure that you are using an equivalent weight of yarn. When knitting the project, use the needle size stated in the pattern; this may differ from that recommended by the manufacturer in order to achieve a particular look.

4 If felting is included in the pattern, check to see that the substituted yarn fibers are suitable—that is, not cotton, superwash wool, or synthetic.

Beads and sequins

Beads and sequins can add a touch of glamour to a knitted garment and are great for embellishing jewelry. When choosing beads, check whether or not they are machine washable. Also take into consideration the weight of yarn you are using. For example, do not use large glass beads on a light-weight fabric because they will cause the knitting to sag.

Sequins are usually made of plastic, so avoid dry cleaning, pressing, or steaming them. Round sequins can be either flat or cupped—that is, the edges are faceted and tilt up toward the central hole. Take care when using the cupped variety that they face away from the surface of the knitting or their edges can damage the yarn.

Buttons and buckles

Buttons can make or break a project, so it is worth spending a little more for an interesting button that will enhance your knitted piece. Always buy buttons after working the buttonholes to ensure a good fit. Follow the same advice for buckles.

Other materials

Other materials used to make the projects in this book include: a pillow form, zipper, pin clip, key chain clip, leather thonging, polyester fibrefill, and embroidery thread. These can all be purchased from good craft stores.

Equipment

All you need to get started is some yarn and a pair of knitting needles. As your skills progress, however, you will find that you need some additional equipment. It is a good idea to build up your collection as you go, rather than trying to get everything together before you knit your first piece.

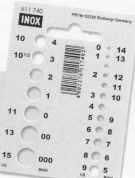

Needle gauge

This is very useful for checking or converting needle sizes, especially since the numbers printed on the needles can wear off with age.

Straight needles

These come in pairs and a range of sizes. Knitting needles are made from a variety of materials, including plastic, aluminum, bamboo, wood, and steel. The cheapest are plastic and aluminum. Bamboo and wooden needles are more expensive, but give a much more pleasurable knitting experience. An inexpensive way to build your needle collection is by scouring thrift shops, where you will often find whole sets of needles for sale. It is important to use the right size of needle for the yarn you are using and the project you are making. Each pattern tells you which size to use.

Circular needles

Circular needles consist of two short needles joined by a flexible length of nylon cord. They come in different sizes and the length of cord varies. Although normally used for working in the round, circular needles can also be used for straight knitting, which is especially useful when you have too many stitches for a straight knitting needle or your work is heavy.

Double-pointed needles

Double-pointed needles come in sets of four or five and are generally used for knitting socks and gloves. Having points at each end, they enable you to knit from either end of the needle.

Cable needles

These short double-pointed needles are used to hold stitches at the front or back of work when working cable patterns. They can be straight or U-shaped and come in three sizes. Choose the size that is closest to the main needle size, so that it does not stretch the stitches (slightly smaller is better than too big).

Stitch holder

Like large safety pins, these are used to hold stitches—for example, at a neckline. If you are caught without one, thread a contrasting colored yarn through the stitches and knot the ends together, then slip the stitches off the needle.

Tape measure

This is essential for measuring your work and test swatches.

Scissors

A small, sharp pair of scissors is essential, although it is better to break woolen yarns because the feathered ends from breaking are easier to hide when weaving in.

Row counter

This fits neatly on the end of a needle. Turn the dial as you work each row.

Sewing needles

Blunt-ended tapestry needles come with different size eyes to accommodate various thicknesses of yarn. They are essential for sewing seams and weaving in loose ends of yarn. Sharp sewing needles are needed to sew on sequins and beads.

Glass-headed pins

Use these to hold pieces of knitting together when sewing up and blocking and pressing. They are also useful for marking button positions.

Safety pins

These can be used as stitch holders if only a few stitches need to be held, or as stitch markers if you do not have any. They are also handy for catching a dropped stitch until you can pick it up.

Stitch markers

These colored plastic or metal rings are useful for marking a stitch or row. They are also handy when you need to cast on a larger number of stitches to prevent you from losing count.

Notebook

Keep a small notebook handy to record where you are in the pattern or any changes you have made.

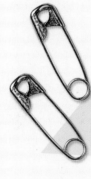

Getting started

The first step when beginning to knit is to create a foundation row of loops called a cast-on. It is also important to hold the needles and yarn correctly. There are numerous ways of doing this, but the best method is the one that feels most comfortable to you.

Holding the yarn

A good technique for holding the yarn is to wrap it around the little finger, then snake it around the other fingers in a way that feels comfortable. This tensions the yarn so that it travels smoothly and evenly as it passes through your hands, while leaving your fingertips free to control the needles. You can hold the yarn in your left or right hand. Holding the yarn in the left hand is faster because the yarn does not have as far to travel to work each stitch.

Holding the needles

Needles can be held from above, known as the "knife hold," or from beneath, known as the "pen hold." The left needle is always held from above, while the right needle can be held either way.

American method

With this method, both needles are held from above in the knife hold. The right hand controls the yarn and moves the right needle into and out of the stitches on the left needle, while the left hand moves the stitches on the left needle.

Continental method

This is the fastest method of knitting. Both needles are held from above in the knife hold. The left hand controls the yarn and moves the stitches on the left needle, while the right hand moves the right needle into and out of the stitches on the left needle.

Scottish method

With this method, both needles are held from above in the knife hold. The left hand controls the needles, moving the stitches toward the tip of the left needle to be worked and guiding the right needle into and out of the stitches. The right needle is supported under the right arm, while the right hand controls the feed of the yarn.

French method

This style of knitting is considered to be elegant but time-consuming. The left needle is held from above in the knife hold, while the right needle is held from beneath in the pen hold between the thumb and index finger. The right index finger is used to guide the yarn around the needles.

Casting on

There are several ways of doing this, but the cable cast-on described here produces a firm but elastic edge that is suitable for most purposes. The first step is to make a slipknot.

Making a slipknot

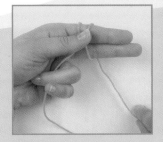 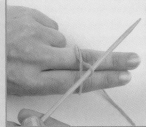 

1 Unwind a few inches (cm) from the yarn ball. With the short end of yarn hanging inside your palm, wrap the long end (attached to the ball) clockwise once around the first two fingers of your left hand. Use the left thumb to hold the yarn circle in place on top of the left index finger.

2 With a knitting needle in your right hand, insert the needle through the center of the yarn circle and pull up a loop of the long end (attached to the ball).

3 Release the yarn from your left hand and gently pull on both ends to firm up the knot, then pull on the long end to tighten the loop around the needle. If you pulled too hard and the loop is too tight, gently pull on the short end to loosen. This is your first stitch.

Cable cast-on

1 Hold the needle with the slipknot in your left hand, then insert the right needle into the slipknot from front to back underneath the left needle. Wrap the yarn counterclockwise around the tip of the right needle.

2 Use the right needle to pull the new loop of yarn through the slipknot.

3 Place this new stitch on the left needle, then remove the right needle and gently pull the long end of the yarn (this is now called the working yarn) to tighten the stitch around the needle.

4 *Insert the right needle between the first two stitches on the left needle. Wrap the yarn around the right needle same as before, pull up a new loop, and place this stitch on the left needle. Continue making stitches this way, repeating instructions from *, until you have the number of stitches called for.

Tips

If your cast-on is too tight, control this by inserting the right needle between the first two stitches on the left needle before you tighten the yarn of the previous stitch. The needle circumference held between the stitches before tightening the yarn each time will help prevent the cast-on from becoming too tight. Or, try casting on with a larger needle. You can also produce a looser cast-on by inserting the right needle into the loop of the last stitch made, rather than between the last two stitches. However, this alters the cast-on method to one called the knit cast-on, so use either method, but don't use both methods together. If your cast-on is too loose, try casting on with a smaller needle. When knitting the first row after casting on, it sometimes helps to knit into the back of the stitches. This tightens up the cast-on edge.

Knit and purl

All knitted fabrics are created using these two stitches in various combinations. Always hold the yarn at the back of the work for a knit stitch and at the front of the work for a purl stitch unless instructed otherwise in the pattern.

The knit stitch

1 With yarn in back of the work, hold the needle with the stitches in your left hand and insert the right needle through the first stitch on the left needle from front to back. The right needle will be beneath the left needle.

2 Wrap the yarn counterclockwise around the tip of the right needle.

3 Use the right needle to pull the wrapped yarn toward you, moving through the stitch on the left needle, and forming a new stitch on the right needle. Slip the original stitch off the left needle. Continue in this way until all the stitches in the row have been worked onto the right needle.

The purl stitch

1 With yarn in front of the work, hold the needle with the stitches in your left hand and insert the right needle through the first stitch on the left needle from right to left. The right needle will be closest to you and in front of the left needle.

2 Wrap the yarn counterclockwise around the tip of the right needle.

3 Use the right needle to pull the wrapped yarn through the stitch on the left needle, moving slightly upward and away from you, and forming a new stitch on the right needle. Slip the original stitch off the left needle. Continue in this way until all the stitches in the row have been worked onto the right needle.

Stitch patterns

By combining knit and purl stitches in different ways, you can create a variety of textured fabrics. The most frequently used are garter stitch, stockinette stitch, reverse stockinette stitch, ribbing, and seed stitch.

Garter stitch

This is the simplest stitch pattern and creates a reversible fabric that does not curl, making it ideal for scarves, borders, and edges. Cast on the required number of stitches.
Row 1: Knit.
Repeat row 1 until the required length is achieved.

Stockinette stitch

Stockinette stitch is the most well-known combination of knit and purl, producing a smooth, flat fabric on the right side of the work. Cast on the required number of stitches.
Row 1 (right side): Knit.
Row 2 (wrong side): Purl.
Repeat rows 1–2 until the required length is achieved.

Reverse stockinette stitch

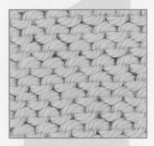

This is the same as stockinette stitch but uses the ridged purl side of the fabric as the right side, instead of the smooth knit side. It is often used as a background for cables in order to make the cables more pronounced. Cast on the required number of stitches.
Row 1 (right side): Purl.
Row 2 (wrong side): Knit.
Repeat rows 1–2 until the required length is achieved.

Ribbing

This stitch makes a very elastic fabric that is mainly used for neckbands and edgings. It is worked by alternating knit and purl stitches along each row to produce vertical lines of stitches on both sides of the work. The two most common ribs are single rib (k1, p1), pictured top, and double rib (k2, p2), pictured above. For single rib, cast on an even number of stitches.
Row 1: *K1, p1, repeat from * to end.
Repeat row 1 until the required length is achieved. For double rib, cast on a multiple of four stitches.
Row 1: *K2, p2, repeat from * to end.
Repeat row 1 until the required length is achieved.

Seed stitch

This creates a firmly textured, reversible fabric. It is formed in the same way as ribbing by alternating knit and purl stitches on each row, but instead of aligning the stitches in vertical columns, they are worked so that purl stitches sit on top of knit stitches and knits on top of purls. If worked over an odd number of stitches, you can start and finish each row with a knit stitch.

Cast on an odd number of stitches.
Row 1: K1, *p1, k1, repeat from * to end.
Repeat row 1 until the required length is achieved. If the instructions specify an even number of stitches, then two rows are repeated. Cast on even number of stitches.
Row 1: *K1, p1, repeat from * to end.
Row 2: *P1, k1, repeat from * to end.
Repeat rows 1–2 until the required length is achieved.

Binding off

Once you have finished your knitting, you need to secure the stitches by binding them off. Binding off is also used to finish a group of stitches to shape the work. The bound-off edge should stretch about as much as the rest of the knitting. Throughout the projects, you will be asked to bind off knitwise, purlwise, or in pattern.

Binding off knitwise

1 Knit the first two stitches in the usual way.

2 Insert the tip of the left needle, from left to right, through the front of the first stitch on the right needle. Lift the first stitch over the second stitch and off the right needle. You have bound off one stitch.

3 Knit the next stitch so that you have two stitches on the right needle again. Repeat step 2 to bind off another stitch, then continue this process to bind off as many stitches as required.

4 When binding off all the stitches in a row, you will end up with a single stitch on the right needle. Cut the yarn, leaving a tail of about 6" (15 cm). Slip the final stitch off the right needle, thread the tail of yarn through it, and pull tight to secure.

Knitwise bind-off

Purlwise bind-off

Double rib bind-off

Binding off purlwise or in pattern

When binding off purl stitches, simply purl the first two stitches as usual and follow the instructions for binding off knitwise, purling stitches instead of knitting them and keeping the yarn at the front of the work. To lift each stitch off the right needle, insert the left needle into the back of the stitch, from left to right. When binding off a piece worked in rib or another textured stitch pattern, keep the appearance consistent by working each stitch as knit or purl according to the stitch pattern.

Tip

When binding off a certain number of stitches, to shape a neck for example, always count the stitches as you lift them off the needle, not as you work them. The stitch remaining on the right needle does not count as a bound-off stitch—it is either secured as stated above, or becomes the first stitch in the next set of instructions.

Gauge

Most knitting patterns specify an ideal gauge, which is the number of stitches and rows counted over a certain measurement, usually 4" (10 cm) square, worked in a specified stitch pattern and needle size. If you do not work to the correct gauge, the knitting will end up the wrong size. This is not important for some projects, such as the felted buttons, but it is crucial to get the gauge right when knitting items such as garments.

Making a test swatch

Using the recommended needle size, cast on the number of stitches specified in the gauge guide plus four more. If the stitches are to be measured over a pattern, cast on the correct multiple of stitches to knit the pattern. Work in the required pattern until the swatch measures approximately 5" (12.5 cm) square. Cut the yarn, thread it through the stitches, and slip them off the needle. Do not pull the yarn tight or bind off because this may distort the stitches.

Adjusting your gauge

Too tight   Correct gauge   Too loose

If you have fewer stitches than stated in the gauge guide, your knitting is too loose and the garment will be too big. Knit another swatch using smaller needles. If you have more stitches than stated in the gauge guide, your knitting is too tight and the garment will be too small. Knit another swatch using larger needles. This should give you the correct gauge if you are off by only one or two stitches. However, if the difference is greater, you may need to adjust the size of garment that you make.

Although a difference of two or three stitches may seem minor, remember that this is two or three stitches in just 4" (10 cm). Think how many 4" (10 cm) there are across the width of your garment. For example, if the gauge should be 20 stitches and yours is 22 stitches to 4" (10 cm), a garment measuring 24" (60 cm) has six lots of 4" (10 cm), so your garment will be off by 12 stitches. This means your garment will only measure approximately 22" (55 cm) and could be too small or an uncomfortable fit.

Counting stitches and rows

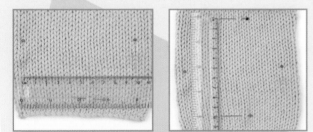

Lay the swatch on a flat surface. Place a ruler horizontally in the center of the swatch and measure 4" (10 cm). Mark this distance with two pins. Count the number of stitches between the pins, including half stitches, if any. Make sure you are accurate, because even half a stitch difference could make the finished garment the wrong size. Repeat the process vertically to count the number of rows.

> ### Tip
> Depending on the yarn and stitch pattern, you may find it easier to turn the test swatch over and measure the rows on the reverse side.

Patterns and charts

The instructions for knitting a project may be provided in either written or chart form, or a combination of both. Always read the whole pattern before you start knitting to ensure that you have everything you need and understand all the instructions.

Essential information

All patterns provide a list containing the size of the finished item, the materials and tools required, the gauge of the piece, and the abbreviations used in the instructions. Although many abbreviations are standardized, such as k for knit and p for purl, some of them vary, so always read the abbreviations before you start knitting.

Abbreviations

Abbreviations are used to save space and make written patterns easier to follow. The abbreviations used in this book are:

2/2RC—cable 2 stitches to the right
3/3RC—cable 3 stitches to the right
BO—bind off
k1f&b—knit into front and back of stitch
k—knit
m1—make 1 stitch
ML—make loop
p1f&b—purl into front and back of stitch
p—purl
psso—pass slip stitch over
RS—right side
skpo—slip 1 stitch, knit 1 stitch, pass slip stitch over
sl 1—slip 1 stitch
ssk—slip 2 stitches knitwise, then knit them together
st(s)—stitch(es)
tbl—through back of loop
tog—together
WS—wrong side
wyb—take yarn between needles to back of work
wyf—bring yarn between needles to front of work
yo—yarnover

Repeats

When following the pattern instructions, you will find that some of them appear within curved parentheses and some are marked with an asterisk. Instructions that appear within parentheses are to be repeated. For example, instead of writing "p2, k2, p2, k2," the pattern will simply say "(p2, k2) twice." Asterisks (*) indicate the point to which you should return when you reach the phrase "repeat from *." They may also mark whole sets of instructions that are to be repeated. For example, "repeat from * to **" means repeat the instructions between the single and double asterisks.

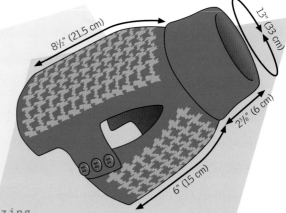

Sizing

Most garment patterns are written for more than one size; in this book the smallest size is shown first, with subsequent sizes in brackets—for example, small [medium, large]. This format is repeated throughout a pattern for all the sets of figures that differ from one size to the next—for example, the number of stitches to cast on. Follow the instructions for the size you are making. Where only one figure is given, this applies to all sizes. Some patterns also include a small schematic drawing, such as the houndstooth dog coat pictured above, showing the actual measurements and general shape of the finished pieces. These are useful reference when blocking pieces and sewing them together.

Charts

Charts are a graphic representation of your knitting, with each square representing one stitch and each horizontal line representing one row. All charts have a key nearby to explain each of the symbols and/or colors used. Charts have several advantages over row-by-row written instructions: you can see where you are at a glance; you learn to plan ahead, especially in color knitting; and they help to increase your understanding of knitting. Always remember that charts are read from the bottom up. Right side (RS) rows are read from right to left; wrong side (WS) rows are read from left to right. The chart indicates how the work appears on the right side. The sample charts pictured below are used to make the houndstooth dog coat.

Tips

If you are new to working from charts, you may find it helpful to enlarge them on a photocopier to make them easier to follow. It is also a good idea to mark off each row as you go. When knitting a garment that has different instructions for different sizes, you may find it easier to follow if you highlight the instructions for the particular size you are making.

Lower panel chart

Key

▥	Yarn A
✚	Yarn B
☐	Repeat frame

Upper panel chart

Shaping techniques

To shape your knitting—for example, along armholes, neck, and sleeve edges—there are various techniques for increasing and decreasing the number of stitches to make the knitting wider or narrower.

Increases

Increases are worked to make the knitted fabric wider by adding to the number of stitches. The simplest way is to work into the front and back of a stitch (abbreviated as k1f&b or p1f&b), while the make 1 method (abbreviated as m1) will create an invisible increase.

Tip

Work increases and decreases one stitch in from the edges of the fabric. This creates a neater edge and makes sewing seams and picking up stitches (around necklines, for example) easier and neater.

Working into front and back of stitch

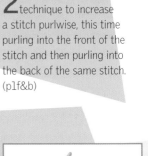

1 Knit into the front of the stitch in the usual way, but do not slip the stitch off the left needle. Knit into the back loop of the same stitch, then slip the stitch off the needle. (k1f&b)

2 You can use the same technique to increase a stitch purlwise, this time purling into the front of the stitch and then purling into the back of the same stitch. (p1f&b)

Make 1

1 Insert the tip of the right needle from front to back beneath the horizontal bar of yarn between two stitches where you want the increase. Slip the bar onto the left needle (pictured), then create a new stitch by knitting through the back of the loop. This twists the loop and prevents making a hole. (m1 knitwise)

2 You can use the same technique to make a stitch purlwise, this time purling through the back of the loop. (m1 purlwise)

Decreases

Decreases are used to make the fabric narrower by reducing the number of stitches. Various techniques are used, depending on whether the decrease needs to slope to the right (abbreviated as k2tog or p2tog) or to the left (abbreviated as k2tog tbl, p2tog tbl, ssk, skpo, or ssp).

Sloping to the right

1 To decrease a stitch knitwise, insert the right needle from left to right through the first two stitches on the left needle, entering the second stitch first, and then the first stitch. Knit them together as a single stitch, then drop them off the left needle. (k2tog)

2 To decrease a stitch purlwise, insert the right needle into the front loop of the first two stitches on the left needle, entering both from right to left, the first stitch followed by the second one. Purl them together as a single stitch, then drop them off the left needle. (p2tog)

Sloping to the left

1 To decrease a stitch knitwise, slip two stitches, one at a time, from the left needle to the right needle; insert the left needle tip from left to right through the front loop of both stitches, then knit them together from this position. (ssk)

2 Another method of decreasing a stitch knitwise is to insert the right needle from right to left through the back loops of two stitches on the left needle, entering the first stitch then the second stitch. Knit them together as a single stitch, then drop them off the left needle. (k2tog tbl)

3 A third method of decreasing a stitch knitwise is to slip the first stitch from the left to the right needle without working it. Knit the next stitch in the usual way, then pass the slipped stitch over the knitted stitch as if binding off. (skpo)

4 To decrease a stitch purlwise, insert the right needle from left to right through the back loops of the first two purl stitches on the left needle, entering the second stitch first, and then the first stitch, both stitches will be twisted. Purl them together as a single stitch, then drop them off the left needle. This can be a little awkward to work. This decrease slopes to the left when viewed from the knit side of the work. (p2tog tbl)

5 To decrease a stitch purlwise with untwisted stitches, slip two purl stitches knitwise, one at a time, from the left needle to the right needle. Slip both stitches back to the left needle, purlwise, (the two stitches will be twisted at this point), then purl both together through the back loops (this will untwist the base of both stitches). (ssp)

Tip

When working necklines and armholes that need to decrease symmetrically on each side, use one method at the beginning of the row and another at the end of the row. This creates what is called "fully fashioned" marks. For example, to make stitches that slope toward the center of the garment, ssk or skpo at the beginning of the row, then k2tog at the end of the row. To make stitches that slant toward the edges of the garment, k2tog at the beginning of the row, then ssk or k2tog tbl at the end of the row.

Other techniques

Having learned the basics of knitting, purling, and shaping, you will find that there are many variations on these instructions used in knitting patterns to create specific effects.

Slipping stitches

Many techniques involve slipping stitches from one needle to another without working them. The way that a stitch is slipped will determine the way that it sits on the needle, so it will need to be slipped knitwise or purlwise.

1 To slip a stitch knitwise, insert the tip of the right needle into the stitch on the left needle as if to knit it. Slip the stitch from the left to the right needle without working into it. The stitch is now on the right needle in a twisted position. When stitches are slipped knitwise, they are transferred to the right needle in a twisted position; this means the back leg of the stitch is now in front of the needle, closest to the knitter. Some stitch techniques require this, others do not.

2 Use the same technique to slip a stitch purlwise, but insert the right needle into the stitch on the left needle as if to purl it. The stitch remains in its normal position, untwisted.

Rule of thumb
Always slip stitches purlwise, unless the instructions state otherwise. The exception to this rule is when a stitch is part of a decrease (skpo, ssk, etc); then the stitches are slipped knitwise. When the decrease is completed, the stitches will be untwisted.

Yarnovers

This involves taking the yarn over the right needle to create a lace hole. Depending on the next stitch, the pattern will instruct you to bring the yarn to the front (wyf—with yarn forward) or take the yarn back (wyb—with yarn back) so that you have to wrap the yarn over the needle to make the next stitch, thereby creating the hole.

1 This example shows a yarnover between two knit stitches. Instead of knitting the second stitch with the yarn at the back of the work in the usual way, the yarn is passed between the needles to the front of the work, then taken over the right needle to knit the next stitch.

2 This yarnover is between two purl stitches. The yarn begins in front, then is taken over the right needle to the back, then passed between the needles to the front of the work again to purl the next stitch as usual.

3 This example shows a yarnover between a knit and a purl stitch. Bring the yarn to the front between the needles, then take the yarn over the right needle to the back, then between the needles to the front again, and purl the next stitch as usual.

4 This example shows a yarnover between a purl and a knit stitch. Leave the yarn in front of the work, then knit the next stitch, taking the yarn over and toward the back of the right needle as the next stitch is knit.

Joining new yarn

Whenever a ball of yarn is about to run out, join a new one at the beginning of a row. When possible, avoid joining a new ball of yarn in the middle of a row.

1 To help keep good tension when starting a new yarn, tie it around the original yarn (the knot can be untied when you are weaving in the ends of yarn after you have finished the piece). Without breaking or cutting the yarn used for the previous row, tie the new yarn around the end of the old yarn, leaving a 6" (15 cm) tail.

2 Slide the knot up to the next stitch and work the row using the new yarn. Hold the tail of yarn out of the way for the first few stitches, then break or cut the old yarn, leaving a tail long enough to weave in later.

Holding stitches

Some projects require stitches to be left on a holder and worked at a later stage in the pattern.

1 To transfer stitches to a stitch holder, simply insert the pin of the holder from right to left through each stitch on the left needle, or from left to right through each stitch on the right needle, taking care not to twist them.

2 Close the holder. The stitches will not unravel. When you need to work on these stitches again, slip them from the holder onto a knitting needle, taking care not to twist them.

Cabling

A cable is made by crossing one set of stitches over another. The cables may cross to the left or to the right. In order to work the cable, a third (cable) needle is used to hold the stitches to be moved, either at the back or front of the work, depending on the direction in which the cable is crossing. Using a cable needle slightly smaller in size than the main needles will help to avoid stretching the stitches.

Right-cross cable   **Left-cross cable**

1 Slip the specified number of stitches off the left needle onto the cable needle and hold the cable needle at the back of the work. Work the next stitches from the left needle as instructed.

1 Work as for a right-cross cable but hold the stitches on the cable needle at the front of the work instead of at the back.

2 Bring the cable needle into knitting position and work the stitches from the cable needle as instructed. You have now finished with the cable needle. Continue the row working from the left needle as instructed in the pattern.

2 Work the stitches from the left needle and then from the cable needle as instructed in the pattern. The finished cable crosses to the left.

Picking up stitches

Many knitted pieces have a border of some kind to neaten the edge and prevent the fabric from curling. These can be knitted separately and sewn onto the piece, or they can be worked by picking up stitches along the edge and working them. Stitches must be picked up evenly, particularly around areas such as necklines that will be a focal point. You can pick up stitches using a knitting needle or a crochet hook. For a neater appearance, use a knitting needle or crochet hook 1 or 2 sizes smaller than the project size to pick up the stitches. If the border is worked in another color than the body of the piece, it can look better if you pick up the stitches in the main color and then change yarn colors for the first row.

Note

There are two methods that refer to picking up stitches. The standard method picks up a stitch and uses the working yarn to make a new stitch at the same time. The second method simply slides the needle under a stitch and slips it onto the needle, without using the working yarn. The loops picked up are snug, and not to gauge. When the pick-up is complete, the yarn is joined to the work and the first row or round begins knitting or purling the stitches according to the instructions. The method we describe below is the pick up and knit method, using the working yarn at the same time.

Marking the edge

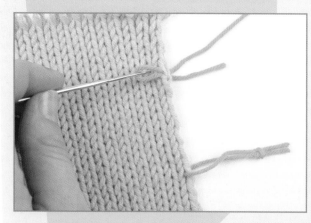

*Measure the edge of the knitted piece and place markers or short knotted pieces of yarn at regular intervals, such as every 2" (5 cm). To calculate how many stitches to pick up between the markers, divide the number of stitches required by the number of sections. For example, if you need to pick up 20 stitches along a 10" (25.5 cm) edge that has been divided into five 2" (5 cm) sections, you will need to pick up four stitches in each section.

Picking up along a horizontal edge

When picking up stitches along a horizontal edge, insert the right needle tip into the center of the first full stitch below the bind-off row. Do not pick up stitches in the bind-off row, otherwise the pick-up row may appear to be a half-stitch off when compared to stitches in the rows below. When picking up stitches along the cast-on edge, work the pick-up one full row above the cast-on edge, or as specified in the instructions.

1 With the right side of the work facing you, insert the right needle (or crochet hook) from front to back through the center of the stitch.

2 Wrap the yarn around the needle as if to knit and pull the loop through to the front of the work to create a new stitch on the right needle. If using a crochet hook, slip the new loop onto the right needle. Do this for as many stitches as required.

Picking up along a vertical edge

When picking up stitches along a vertical edge, work one full stitch in from the edge of the knitted piece.

1 With the right side of the work facing you, insert the right needle from front to back into the first full stitch of the first row—that is, one whole stitch in from the edge.

2 Wrap the yarn around the needle as if to knit and pull the loop through to the front of the work to create a new stitch on the right needle. Repeat for as many stitches as required.

Picking up along a shaped edge

When picking up stitches on any piece of shaped knitting, pick up one stitch in from the edge to eliminate jagged or untidy shaping. Follow the line of the curve, and avoid picking up stitches in any large gaps between bound-off stitches or decreases.

Tips

Stitches that were placed on stitch holders or not bound off (center front neckline, for example) are likely to have stretched loopy stitches at each end. To neaten these areas and prevent a hole, use one of the following methods. Work into the back loop of the offending stitch, thereby twisting it and tightening the stitch to match the others. Or, if the stitch is very loose, slip the stitch knitwise onto the right needle, insert the left needle from back to front under the running strand, pull up a loop, and slip it knitwise onto the right needle, then work both the stitch and loop together using the ssk decrease method.

Buttonholes

This versatile buttonhole is worked over two rows, with a number of stitches bound off on the first row and then cast on again on the second row.

1 Work to the position of the buttonhole. Bind off the required number of stitches, then continue following the pattern instructions.

2 Work to the point of the bound-off stitches, then turn the work and cast on the required number of stitches using the cable cast-on method. Slip the last cast-on stitch onto the left needle. Turn the work again, and continue following the pattern instructions. Repeat for each buttonhole.

Picking up dropped stitches in stockinette stitch

If you drop any stitches, pick them up as soon as you notice and before binding off.

1 With the knit side of the work facing you, insert a crochet hook into the dropped stitch from the front.

2 Pick up the first horizontal strand of unraveled yarn above the dropped stitch and pull it through the stitch to the front.

3 Continue doing this until all the unraveled strands have been picked up, turning the work so that the knit side is facing you if necessary. Transfer the stitch back onto the left knitting needle when you have finished.

Tip

When working the second buttonhole row, at the last cast-on stitch, bring the yarn to the front of the work, traveling between the last stitch on the left needle and the loop on the right needle, then slip the loop from the right needle onto the left needle (the last cast-on stitch of the buttonhole). This will prevent a hole with a long running strand from forming between the end of the buttonhole and the following work, and creates a neat buttonhole.

Color work

Working with color adds a new dimension to plain knitting. The simplest way to introduce color is to work in stripes. However, it is also possible to work with more than one color in a row by using Fair Isle, color stranding, or intarsia techniques, all of which are usually created by following a chart.

Fair Isle

Traditional Fair Isle uses no more than two colors in a row to form a pattern. Although the colors may change often within the row, and other colors introduced on subsequent rows, the rule of no more than two colors per row still applies. The yarns in use are carried across the wrong side of the work, creating a double thickness of fabric (or thicker if using more than two colors per row). Over the centuries, knitters have developed numerous methods of carrying multiple yarns simultaneously—too many to mention here. Two standard techniques are described here: stranding and weaving in. True Fair Isle designs, worked in fine-gauge woolen yarns, are usually small and seldom require weaving-in. However, in current knitting terms, Fair Isle is often used as a generic name applied to many color-stranded knitting methods, regardless of the pattern size or the number of colors used in a single row. These methods generally require both stranding and weaving-in because the pattern or motif is often larger, and generally, thicker yarns are used.

Stranding

Stranding is where a color that is not being used is carried across the back of the work during short floats without being anchored using a technique such as weaving-in. Care must be taken to avoid pulling the stranded yarns too tightly across the back, otherwise the knitted fabric will pucker.

1 One hand: The yarns are held in one hand, dropping one color while the other color is in use (this is the slowest method, but easiest for someone new to color knitting). If the knitter has more dexterity and patience, a faster method is draping the background color (A) over the index finger, and the pattern color (B) over the middle finger, and bringing the correct finger/color forward to wind the yarn around the needle when a color is used.

2 Two hands: Both yarns are carried at the same time, with the background color (A) held in the right hand, and the pattern color (B) in the left hand (this method is said to be the fastest, but becomes a little tricky if more than two colors are used per row).

Note
When stranding two yarns, the most important thing to remember is consistency. In the one-hand method, always strand the background color (A) over the pattern color (B), and the pattern color (B) under the background color (A). In the two-hand method, the background color (A, held in the right hand) strands over the pattern color (B, held in the left hand), or vice versa if you prefer. Follow the same formula throughout the garment. If you switch hands and colors within the garment, the pattern color may recede and the background color become more dominant; the difference in your garment will be highly visible.

Weaving-in

Weaving-in is one method used to anchor the yarn not in use during long floats, and the method can be used in every stitch until the next change of color. However, this has disadvantages; it is slower to weave in every stitch, and the woven color is often noticeable on the right side of the work, especially if highly contrasting colors are used. In today's knitting, a single woven-in stitch is usually made about every inch-worth (2.5 cm) of stitches, and helps to avoid the disadvantages. For the techniques illustrated below, yarn A is held in the right hand and yarn B in the left hand. When you work color-stranding circularly (in rounds), it will not be necessary to use the purl-stitch weave-in, because every row is knit.

Tips

Always carry the yarn not in use to the end of each row or you will end up with a single thickness at the edges. Be careful when choosing colors for Fair Isle because heavily contrasting colors can show through to the front of the work when woven in at the back.

1 On the knit side, place the right needle up through the next stitch on the left needle from left to right and under yarn B on the left forefinger.

2 Knit the next stitch using yarn A, dropping both yarns from the left needle as you do so. Use your left forefinger to keep yarn B taut at the reverse of the work while you knit the next stitch.

3 On the purl side, hold yarn B in place at the front of the work, using your left thumb. Place the right needle through the next stitch from right to left and under yarn B.

4 Purl the next stitch using the right needle, being careful not to push both colors through the center of the stitch.

Weaving-in and stitch gauge

When to anchor the yarn not in use really depends on the stitch gauge. For example, if the stitch gauge in one garment equals 10 stitches to the inch (a very fine yarn), then you do not need to weave in the yarn every 2 or 3 stitches. At that gauge, the stranding distance over 2 or 3 stitches is too short to worry about snags. However, if the project gauge is 4 or 5 stitches to the inch, then you would certainly want to consider anchoring the unused yarn about every 2 or 3 stitches to prevent snags. If the project specified working 11 stitches with yarn A, and the gauge was 5 stitches/one inch (2.5 cm), you would probably weave in yarn B after knitting 3 or 4 stitches, and again after stitches 8 or 9 of the 11 stitches. If you were working at 10 stitches per inch, then anchoring the unused yarn after 5 stitches would be sufficient. Always consider the stitch gauge first, and then make your own decision about when to weave-in. Doing so too frequently distorts the shape of the knitted stitch; doing so less frequently creates long strands across the wrong side of the work that could snag.

Intarsia

This technique is worked with a separate strand of yarn color for each color block, producing a single thickness of fabric. Each color is joined at the appropriate point in the row, and linked with the adjacent color by twisting them around each other on the wrong side. This is done to avoid gaps in the knitting. It is essential that the gauge is checked for an intarsia pattern, because this may vary from single-color stockinette stitch if both are used in same pattern. Intarsia is worked flat, back and forth, because if worked in a true circular fashion, the colors would be at the wrong end of the knitting.

Joining a new color

Tie the new color to the old color leaving a 6" (15-cm) tail to weave in later (you will untie the knot before weaving in the ends). The knot will prevent the stitches from loosening up as you work. Move the knot up close to the needle, insert the right needle into the next stitch on the left needle, bring the new color under the old one, and work the next stitch.

Changing colors

Insert the tip of the right needle into the next stitch (knitwise on a knit row, as here, purlwise on a purl row). Bring the first color over the top of the second color and drop. Pick up the second color (making sure it travels under the first color to keep the yarns twisted) and continue as instructed in the pattern.

Weaving in yarn tails

Stop working and weave in yarn tails from time to time. This will help prevent the yarns from tangling. Untie the joining knot and weave the ends in opposite directions, making sure they remain twisted at the base. This will prevent a hole from occurring between the colors. When possible, avoid weaving one color across another color.

Making bobbins

The simplest way to work intarsia is to cut short, workable lengths of yarn for each motif or block of color and wind them into a neat bobbin. This is much easier than working with full yarn balls, which will become tangled.

1 To calculate how much yarn you need for an area of color, count the number of stitches it occupies and then wrap an end of yarn around the knitting needle you are using for the project the same number of times as there were stitches. This shows you how much yarn the stitches will use, so always allow an extra few inches (cm) to weave in the yarn tails later.

2 Cut the yarn and wind it onto a bobbin if you have a ready made one.

3 If you do not have any bobbins, you can wind a small center-pull ball instead. Hold a 12" (30-cm) tail of yarn under three fingers, open out your thumb and forefinger, and wind the yarn around them in a figure eight.

4 Slip the yarn off your fingers and fold it in half, keeping your thumb over the top of the tail where it enters the ball. Wind the loose yarn around the center of the figure eight to secure it tightly. Tuck the end of the yarn under the last few turns to hold it in place. When using the bobbin, pull on the starting tail to unwind from the center a little at a time.

Finishing

A beautifully knitted garment can easily be ruined by careless finishing. Use a tapestry needle and a length of the yarn that you knitted the project with, and select the method most suitable for the finished effect you want to achieve. Most knitted fabrics need to be blocked before they are stitched together.

Blocking and pressing

Blocking evens out the gauge in the finished work by relaxing the stitches and fixing their size and shape. It also helps edges to life flat without curling. Some fabrics also need to be steamed or pressed.

1 Lay the finished piece with wrong side facing upward onto an ironing board or blocking board. Pin the piece out to the correct dimensions, easing the knitting into shape where necessary.

2 Place a damp cloth over the fabric and press with an iron set at the correct temperature for the yarn used (check the ball band for this information). Do not apply too much pressure or you will flatten the texture of the knitting. For highly textured pieces, hold a steam iron about 1–2" (2–4 cm) above the surface and allow the steam to penetrate the fabric.

3 Do not press or steam synthetics, long-haired yarns or ribbing; simply spray the blocked fabric with water to dampen it, then allow to dry.

Tip
Make your own blocking board by covering a piece of hard board with a layer of padding and an over-layer of cotton fabric. Stretch them tight across the board and secure them to the underside with staples, glue, or tape. Choose a checkered fabric so that you can use the squares as a guide for pinning out pieces with the edges straight.

Weaving in yarn ends

All pieces of knitting begin and end with a tail of yarn, and more are created when you join in a new ball, change colors, and sew up seams. Always leave a tail at least 6" (15 cm) long, so that they can be threaded into a tapestry needle easily and woven into the wrong side of the knitted fabric.

1 Most yarn ends can be woven in along the wrong side of a seam. Weave the needle in and out of the edge stitches of the seam for about 2–3" (5–7.5 cm). Pull the needle through and cut off the excess yarn.

2 Sometimes you will need to weave in the yarn ends along the wrong side of a row either horizontally or diagonally, instead of using a seam, especially in a piece of knitting where there are lots of color changes. Working on the wrong side of the work, weave the needle in and out of the backs of stitches of the same color for 2–3" (5–7.5 cm). Check frequently to make sure the weaving yarn doesn't poke through to the right side of the work. Trim any excess yarn close to the end of the weaving.

Mattress stitch

Also known as invisible horizontal and invisible vertical stitch, this method can be used for any seam and creates a strong, neat, almost invisible join. It is worked with the fabrics laid flat and right sides facing you, so it is ideal when working in stripes or textured patterns because it is easy to pattern match. Variations of this seam can be worked horizontally or vertically. If making a vertical seam, work the seam a half stitch in from the side edge when using heavier weight yarns in order to avoid bulky seams (as shown here); work a whole stitch in from the side edge when using light- and medium-weight yarns.

Tips

It is better to use a separate piece of yarn to sew seams rather than the tail left over from casting on. If you do make a mistake, it can be easily pulled out of the fabric rather than having to unpick it. When using mattress stitch to join a bound-off edge to a side edge, such as when joining a sleeve to an armhole, the number of stitches and the number of rows to be joined will not match exactly, so you may find it easier to pin the seam before stitching, or to start the seam at the center and work along one direction at a time.

Horizontal seam

1 With threaded tapestry needle and beginning in the lower knitted piece and in the row below the bind off, insert the needle into the center of the first side stitch and up through the center of the second stitch.

2 Move the needle to the second knitted piece and above the bind-off row. Insert the needle and thread under both strands of the first stitch.

3 Return to the first knitted piece and insert the needle back into the center of the last stitch worked (the yarn came out of this stitch before moving to the second piece), then bring the needle and yarn out to the front again through the center of the next stitch.

4 Return to the second knitted piece and insert the needle under both strands of the next stitch, as shown. Work the remaining seam repeating steps 3 and 4. When finished, secure both ends of the seam with a couple of overlapping stitches.

Vertical seam

1 Insert threaded tapestry needle under the base and then into the center of the first stitch (or under the horizontal bar between the first 2 stitches).

2 Move across to the adjoining knitted piece and repeat step 1, then return to the first knitted piece and move upward one row and repeat step 1.

3 Repeat this process, zigzagging back and forth between the two side edges and moving upward by one or two rows each time.

4 Gently pull the yarn together every few stitches to close the seam. The seam should appear invisible from the right side. When finished, secure both ends of the seam with a couple of overlapping stitches.

Backstitch

This creates a strong but non-elastic seam and is suitable where firmness is required and for light-weight yarns. It is worked with the wrong sides facing you, so it can be difficult to pattern match exactly. Pin the pieces right sides together, matching the pieces as closely as possible, and keep the stitches near the edge to avoid creating a bulky seam.

Flat seams

When you need to use a stitch that creates as narrow a seam as possible, it is best to use slip stitch or whipstitch. Slip stitch is ideal for attaching any separate pieces to the knitted fabric, such as a pocket, trim, or appliqué, while whipstitch (also known as overcasting) is especially effective on cuffs and collars.

Slip stitch

Whipstitch

1 Secure the seam and yarn by taking the needle twice around the outer edges of the fabric, from back to front.

2 Take the yarn around the outside edge once more, but this time insert the needle through the work from back to front no more than ½" (1.3 cm) from where the yarn last came out.

3 Insert the needle from front to back at the point where the first stitch began, then bring the needle back through to the front, the same distance along the edge as before. Repeat this process along the whole seam, then secure the end with a couple of overlapping stitches.

4 The completed seam, when sewn in matching colored yarn, is strong and neat.

Place the piece to be attached in position with the main work and pin them together. Using a threaded tapestry needle, pull the yarn to the front from the back (leaving a tail at the back to weave in later). *Working from the front of the main piece, pass the threaded needle under the bar of the first stitch to be sewn. Move the needle over to the piece to be attached; then working from the back of that piece, pass the needle under the horizontal bar of the edge of the piece to be attached. Repeat from *, joining the pieces together. As you work, pull the stitches gently about every inch (2.5 cm) or so, in order to prevent the seam from puckering and achieve an even gauge. The seam should match the elasticity of the knitting. When the seam is finished, take the yarn to the wrong side of work and weave the end through several stitches to secure.

Place the knitted pieces right sides together, and pin together about 1" (2.5 cm) from the edge (this leaves you room to hold the work). With threaded needle and wrong sides facing, working as close to the edge of the work as possible, *take the yarn through both thicknesses of fabric from back to front, then over the knitted edge to the back again. Move along the seam edge by a few stitches and repeat from *. Continue joining the pieces together this way along the whole seam. Weave in ends along the seam to secure.

chapter 2

URBAN PLAYGROUND

In this chapter you will find a range of cool knits with a sporty flavor, created using brightly colored cottons and interesting marled blends. Designs range from a simple denim key chain and brightly colored iPod covers to more technically complex kneepad covers and power wristbands. Try the accessories first if you are new to knitting, then progress to the garments when you feel more confident.

Knee-pad covers

These knee-pad covers are for all active skateboarders. Worked in a sturdy DK-weight cotton yarn, they are created in bright colors with attitude. Slip them over the top of the thick pads you should be wearing to protect your knees from knocks and blows, and save your pants from scuffs and scrapes.

THE KNITTY GRITTY

Size: Circumference at widest point: 16" (40 cm).
Yarn: DK-weight cotton (100% cotton; 93 yd [85 m] per 50 g ball): brown (yarn A), 2 balls; turquoise (yarn B), 2 balls.
Needles: Size 5 (3.75 mm). Adjust needle size if necessary to obtain correct gauge.
Notions: Tapestry needle.
Gauge: 20 sts x 28 rows = 4" (10 cm) in stockinette stitch using size 5 (3.75 mm) needles.

Abbreviations
k—knit
p—purl
RS—right side
st(s)—stitch(es)
tbl—through back of loop
tog—together
WS—wrong side
wyb—take yarn between needles to back of work
wyf—bring yarn between needles to front of work

Ribbing

Using size 5 (3.75 mm) needles and yarn A, cast on 86 sts. Join yarn B.
Row 1: (RS) *With yarn B and wyb, k2, with yarn A and wyf, p2; repeat from * to last 2 sts; with yarn B and wyb, k2.
Row 2: *With yarn B and wyf, p2, with yarn A and wyb, k2; repeat from * to last 2 sts, with yarn B and wyf, p2.
Rows 1–2 form the two-color ribbing.
Rows 3–18: Repeat rows 1–2 eight times.

Kneecap shaping (increasing)

Row 19: Rib 40, k8 using yarn A, break off yarn B, turn.
Continue using yarn A.
Row 20: P10, turn work leaving remaining sts on needle.
Row 21: K12, turn.
Row 22: P14, turn.
Row 23: K16, turn.
Row 24: P18, turn.
Row 25: K20, turn.
Row 26: P22, turn.
Row 27: K24, turn.
Row 28: P26, turn.
Row 29: K28, turn.
Row 30: P30, turn.
Row 31: K32, turn.
Row 32: P34, turn.
Row 33: K36, turn.
Row 34: P38, turn.
Row 35: K40, turn.
Row 36: P42, turn.
Row 37: K44, turn.
Row 38: P46, turn.
Row 39: K48, turn.
Row 40: P50, turn.

Kneecap decrease

Row 41: K46, k2tog tbl twice, turn.
Row 42: P44, p2tog twice, turn.
Row 43: K42, k2tog tbl twice, turn.
Row 44: P40, p2tog twice, turn.
Row 45: K38, k2tog tbl twice, turn.
Row 46: P36, p2tog twice, turn.
Row 47: K34, k2tog tbl twice, turn.
Row 48: P32, p2tog twice, turn.

Row 49: K30, k2tog tbl twice, turn.
Row 50: P28, p2tog twice, turn.
Row 51: K26, k2tog tbl twice, turn.
Row 52: P24, p2tog twice, turn.
Row 53: K22, k2tog tbl twice, turn.
Row 54: P20, p2tog twice, turn.
Row 55: K18, k2tog tbl twice, turn.
Row 56: P16, p2tog twice, turn.
Row 57: K14, k2tog tbl twice, turn.
Row 58: P12, p2tog twice, turn.
Row 59: K10, k2tog tbl twice, turn.
Row 60: P8, p2tog twice, turn.

Ribbing

Row 61: K6, k2tog tbl twice, pick up and knit 21 sts along side of kneecap, join yarn B and work 18 sts in two-color ribbing as before (row 1), turn.
Row 62: Work 47 sts in two-color ribbing (row 2), break off yarn B, using yarn A pick up and purl 21 sts from side of kneecap, rejoin yarn B and work 18 sts in two-color ribbing (86 sts).
Rows 63–78: Repeat rows 1–2 eight times.
Bind off knitwise using yarn A.
Repeat to make a second knee pad.

Finishing

With a tapestry needle, weave in the loose yarn tails to WS of work, then steam gently on WS. Sew the back seam using backstitch or mattress stitch, including 1 full stitch from each edge in the seam. After seam is closed, the remaining 2 knit stitches continue the rib pattern sequence.

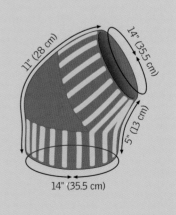

Schematic

11" (28 cm)
14' (35.5 cm)
5" (13 cm)
14" (35.5 cm)

Power wristbands

Wristbands can be worn in winter and summer, and add a feeling of sporty confidence to your day. This Celtic-design pattern is suitable for beginners and is a great introduction to color work. The Fair Isle technique is used here, and involves knitting with more than one color using stockinette stitch; refer to pages 30–32 for guidance on Fair Isle knitting.

Celtic panel

Using size 5 (3.75 mm) needles and yarn A, cast on 18 sts.
Begin chart, working rows 1–13.
Row 1: (RS) Purl.
Row 2: (WS) Purl.
Rows 3–12: Join yarn B, and working both A and B yarns as shown on chart, follow the 10 Celtic design rows, using the Fair Isle technique.
Break off yarn B, leaving a 4" (10 cm) tail.
Row 13: Knit, using yarn A. End of chart rows.
    Bind off knitwise.

Buttonhole panel

Row 1: (RS) Using size 3 (3.25 mm) needles and yarn A, and with the right side of the Celtic panel facing, pick up and knit 11 sts along the 13 rows of one side edge of the panel.
Row 2: *K1, p1, repeat from * to last st, k1. Row 2 forms a seed stitch fabric.
    Repeat row 2 to continue in seed stitch until the panel measures 3" (7.5 cm), ending with a WS row.

Note: When binding off stitches in mid-row, after the second stitch is bound off, there is 1 stitch on the right needle. Because this stitch is already worked and on the right needle, the instructions begin again with the next stitch on the left needle.
Next row (buttonhole row): K1, p1, k1, bind off next 2 sts (1 stitch already on right needle), k1, bind off next 2 sts (1 stitch already on right needle), k1 (7 sts).
Next row: (K1, p1, cast on 2 sts) twice, k1, p1, k1 (11 sts).
Next two rows: Repeat row 2. Bind off in seed stitch.

Button panel

Using size 3 (3.25 mm) needles and yarn A, and with RS of the Celtic panel facing, pick up and knit 11 sts along the remaining side edge of the panel. Work in seed stitch as for the buttonhole panel until the fabric measures 2" (5 cm). Bind off in seed stitch.

Finishing

With a tapestry needle, weave in the loose yarn tails to WS of work. Position the two buttons to correspond with the buttonholes. Check to make sure the fit is comfortable, then sew the buttons in place. Make a second wristband in the same way.

THE KNITTY GRITTY

Size: About 9¼" (23.5 cm) long before overlapping. To make a longer wristband or a headband, add extra rows of seed stitch to the buttonhole and/or button panels.
Yarn: DK-weight cotton (100% cotton; 93 yd [85 cm] per 50 g ball): turquoise (yarn A), 1 ball; brown (yarn B), 1 ball.
Needles: Size 3 (3.25 mm); size 5 (3.75 mm). Adjust needle size if necessary to obtain correct gauge.
Notions: Tapestry needle; four ⅝" (15 mm) buttons; sewing thread and needle if the holes in the buttons are too small to use yarn.
Gauge: 22 sts x 30 rows = 4" (10 cm) in stockinette stitch using size 5 (3.75 mm) needles.

Abbreviations
k—knit
p—purl
RS—right side
st(s)—stitch(es)
WS—wrong side

Celtic panel chart

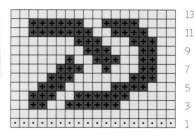

13

11

9

7

5

3

1

☐ Yarn A—k on RS; p on WS

⊡ Yarn A—p on RS

⊞ Yarn B—k on RS; p on WS

Key chain

This essential item for active people will help keep your keys safe and sound no matter what you are doing. No real knitting skills are required for this project. All you have to do is cast on some stitches, then bind them off—it really is that simple. The chain links are put through a washing machine cycle to make the yarn strong and durable, and then finished off with a metal key chain clip.

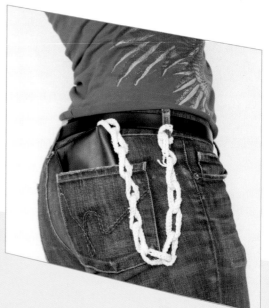

THE KNITTY GRITTY

Size: 19" (48.5 cm) long.
Yarn: DK-weight cotton denim (100% cotton; 102 yd [93 m] per 50 g ball): 1 ball.
Needles: Size 6 (4 mm).
Notions: Tapestry needle; metal key chain clip; zippered lingerie washing bag (optional).
Gauge: Not important.

Abbreviations
st(s)—stitch(es)

Chain links

Using size 6 (4 mm) needles, cast on 10 sts.
Bind off knitwise. Cut yarn, leaving a 6" (15 cm) tail (use this tail later to sew ends together).
This knitted length forms one link of the chain. Make another 12 links in the same way (13 links total).

Finishing

Thread a tapestry needle with 6" (15 cm) tail and sew the ends of the first link together to create a ring. Thread the next link through the ring and then sew the ends of the second link together. Repeat until you have created a chain of 12 links, leaving one link separate and unsewn for attaching the metal clip later. Wash all of the knitted pieces in hot water, but not the metal clip. Optional: Place the links in a zippered lingerie washing bag before placing them inside a washing machine, to keep them together. When dry, thread the metal clip onto the last link, then thread this final link onto the end of the chain and sew the ends of the last link together.

iPod covers

Keep your iPod safe and scratch-free with a knitted iPod cover. The tab top buttons into place to stop the iPod from slipping out, and there is an easy-access hole so that you can reach the control panel with the cover in place. So, not only can you have your own personalized play list, but you can also have a funky cover that will make you stand out from the crowd.

THE KNITTY GRITTY

Size: To fit iPod mini and 20GB iPod.

Yarn: DK-weight cotton (100% cotton; 93 yd [85 m] per 50 g ball): main color (yarn A), 1 ball; contrast color (yarn B), 1 ball.

Needles: Size 3 (3.25 mm). Adjust needle size if necessary to obtain correct gauge.

Notions: Stitch holder; tapestry needle; three ⅝" (15 mm) buttons (one for iPod mini, two for 20GB iPod); sewing thread and needle if the holes in the buttons are too small to use yarn.

Gauge: 16 sts x 25 rows = 4" (10 cm) in seed stitch using size 3 (3.25 mm) needles.

Abbreviations
BO—bind off
k—knit
p—purl
RS—right side
st(s)—stitch(es)
tog—together
WS—wrong side
yo—yarnover

iPod mini

Using size 3 (3.25 mm) needles and yarn B, cast on 16 sts.
Row 1: (RS) *K1, p1, repeat from * to end.
Row 2: *P1, k1, repeat from * to end.
Rows 1–2 form a seed stitch fabric.
Rows 3–4: Repeat rows 1–2, then break off yarn B.
Rows 5–16: Join yarn A, then repeat rows 1–2 six times (12 rows).

Control opening

Row 17: (K1, p1) twice, k1, bind off next 6 sts in pattern; with 1 stitch already on right needle after the BO, work the final 4 stitches from left needle as (k1, p1) twice (10 sts).
Rows 18–22: Working on 5 sts only, (p1, k1) twice, p1 for each row.

Place these 5 sts onto a stitch holder. Rejoin yarn A to the remaining 5 sts with WS facing and (k1, p1) twice, k1 for five rows.
Work the following row across the 5 sts on the needle, cast on 6 sts, and then work the 5 sts from the stitch holder.
Row 23: (K1, p1) twice, k1, cast on 6 sts, (p1, k1) twice, p1 (16 sts).
Row 24: Repeat row 2.
Rows 25–72: Repeat rows 1–2 twenty-four times (48 rows).
Break off yarn A and rejoin yarn B.
Rows 73–76: Repeat rows 1–2 twice (4 rows).
Bind off in seed stitch.
Cut yarn, leaving a tail long enough to sew one seam.

Tab top

Row 1: (RS) With RS facing, pick up and knit 5 sts in the center of the bind-off edge (the back of the iPod cover).
Row 2: (K1, p1) twice, k1.
Row 2 forms a seed stitch fabric.
Rows 3–10: Repeat row 2 eight times (8 rows).
Row 11 (buttonhole row): K1, p1, yo, k2tog, k1 (5 sts).
Row 12: Repeat row 2.
Bind off in seed stitch. Cut yarn, leaving a tail long enough to weave in and secure.

Finishing

With a tapestry needle, weave in the loose yarn tails to the WS of work. Thread the needle with the long yarn tail from the earlier BO row. Fold the cover in half, matching the cast-on and bind-off edges, and sew the first side seam using backstitch or mattress stitch. Rethread the needle for the second side seam. Use a flat seam at the top where yarn B is used to prevent the seam from showing. With the cover right side out, check the correct position for the button, and sew in place with yarn or sewing thread.

20GB iPod
Using size 3 (3.25 mm) needles and yarn B, cast on 19 sts.
Row 1: (RS) *K1, p1, repeat from * to last st, k1.
Row 1 forms a seed stitch fabric.
Rows 2–4: Repeat row 1 three times. Break off yarn B.
Rows 5–22: Join yarn A, then repeat row 1 eighteen times (18 rows).

Control opening
Row 23: (K1, p1) three times, bind off next 7 sts in pattern; with 1 stitch already on right needle after the BO, work the last 5 sts from left needle as (k1, p1) twice, k1 (12 sts).
Working on 6 sts only, work the next nine rows in seed stitch as indicated.
Row 24: (K1, p1) three times.
Row 25: (P1, k1) three times.

Rows 26–32: Repeat rows 24–25 three times, then repeat row 24 once more. Place these 6 sts onto a stitch holder. Rejoin yarn A to the remaining 6 sts with WS facing and work nine rows in seed stitch as indicated.
Row 24: (P1, k1) three times.
Row 25: (K1, p1) three times.
Rows 26–32: Repeat rows 24–25 three times, then repeat row 24 once more. Work the following row across the 6 sts on the needle, cast on 7 sts, and then work the 6 sts from the stitch holder.
Row 33: (K1, p1) three times, cast on 7 sts, (p1, k1) three times (19 sts).

Rest of panel
Rows 34–76: Continue the seed stitch pattern, repeating row 1 (43 rows). Break off yarn A and rejoin yarn B.
Rows 77–80: Repeat row 1. Bind off in seed stitch.

Tab tops
Row 1: (RS) With RS facing, count 3 sts in from the right-hand side and pick up and knit 5 sts from the bind-off edge (the back of the iPod cover).
Row 2: (K1, p1) twice, k1.
Row 2 forms a seed stitch fabric.
Rows 3–9: Repeat row 2 seven times.
Row 10 (buttonhole row): K1, p1, yo, k2tog, k1 (5 sts).
Row 11: Repeat row 2.
Bind off in seed stitch.
Make a second tab to match, counting 8 sts in from the left-hand side as the starting point, and picking up 5 sts, moving toward the left edge with each stitch.

Finishing
Finish as for the iPod mini cover.

Striped beanie

This hat is worked in a two-color stripe using a wool/cotton blend yarn. It is very easy to knit, and provides a good introduction to simple shaping techniques and working with multiple yarns. Although only two colors have been used here, you could use as many as you like. Although the beanie looks great on its own, you could embellish it with funky badges or embroidery patches, as pictured here.

THE KNITTY GRITTY

Size: Adult woman or teens.
Circumference: 20" (51 cm).
Length: About 7" (18 cm).
Yarn: DK-weight blend (50% wool, 50% cotton; 123 yd [113 m] per 50 g ball): green (yarn A), 1 ball; beige (yarn B), 1 ball.
Needles: Size 3 (3.25 mm); size 6 (4 mm). Adjust needle size if necessary to obtain correct gauge.
Notions: Tapestry needle.
Gauge: 22 sts x 32 rows = 4" (10 cm) in stockinette stitch using size 6 (4 mm) needles.

Abbreviations
k—knit
k1f&b—knit into front and back of stitch
p—purl
RS—right side
tog—together
WS—wrong side

Ribbing

Using size 3 (3.25 mm) needles and yarn A, cast on 110 sts.
Row 1: (RS) K2, *p2, k2, repeat from * to end.
Row 2: P2, *k2, p2, repeat from * to end.
Rows 3–4: Join yarn B and repeat rows 1 and 2, using yarn B only.
Rows 5–10: Repeat rows 1–4 once, then rows 1–2 again, remembering to alternate yarns A and B every two rows to maintain the stripe sequence.

Stockinette section

Change to size 6 (4 mm) needles and remember to maintain the stripe sequence throughout.
Rows 11–30: Beginning with a knit row, work 20 rows in stockinette stitch, working k1f&b at the beginning and end of row 11 (112 sts).

Shaping the crown

Row 31: (RS) K1, k2tog, k5, *k2tog, k6, repeat from * to end (98 sts).
Rows 32–34: Work even (without decreases) in stockinette stitch, starting with purl row.
Row 35: (RS) K1, k2tog, k4, *k2tog, k5, repeat from * to end (84 sts).
Rows 36–38: Repeat rows 32–34.
Row 39: (RS) K1, k2tog, k3, *k2tog, k4, repeat from * to end (70 sts).
Rows 40–42: Repeat rows 32–34.
Row 43: (RS) K1, k2tog, k2,* k2tog, k3, repeat from * to end (56 sts).
Rows 44–46: Repeat rows 32–34.

Row 47: (RS) K1, k2tog, k1, *k2tog, k2, repeat from * to end (42 sts).

Rows 48–50: Repeat rows 32–34.

Row 51: (RS) K1, k2tog, *k2tog, k1, repeat from * to end (28 sts).

Rows 52–54: Repeat rows 32–34.

Cut yarn A after finishing last row (row 54), leaving a 4" (10 cm) tail.

Row 55: Using yarn B, *k2tog; repeat from * to end of row (14 sts).

Cut yarn B, leaving a 6" (15 cm) tail. Thread the tail onto a tapestry needle, then insert the the needle and yarn tail through the remaining stitches. Pull yarn tail gently, but firmly, to close top of hat and fasten securely.

Finishing

With a tapestry needle, weave in the loose yarn tails to WS of work, then steam gently on WS. Thread the needle with about 18" (45.5 cm) length of yarn B. Fold the hat in half lengthwise, and sew the back seam using backstitch or mattress stitch.

Carrying yarns up side of work

When using multiple yarns to knit horizontal stripes, you can break off and join the yarns for each stripe, or carry them up the side of the work when not in use. The latter method reduces the number of yarn ends that need to be woven in when you have finished the project. Avoid pulling the yarns too tightly when carrying them up the side because this can cause the edge to distort.

1 After completing the first stripe, drop that color. Pick up the new color from under the old one, insert the right needle into the first stitch, and work the next stripe with the new color according to the instructions.

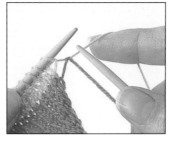

2 For stripes with more than two rows in one color, catch in the unused yarn on every other row by picking up the current yarn from under the unused yarn as you begin the new row.

Schematic

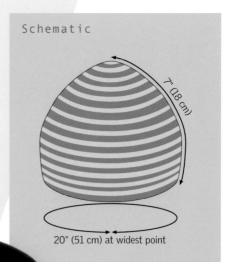

7" (18 cm)

20" (51 cm) at widest point

Hooded top

This hooded top is knitted in a bulky-weight merino/alpaca blend yarn. The broad-stripe bands are worked in stockinette stitch using richly colored marled shades. The baggy hood and the drawstring detail at the bottom make this garment perfect for keeping you wrapped up and cozy on chilly days.

THE KNITTY GRITTY

Size: Small [medium, large]; chest (actual): 39½ [42½, 45½]" (100 [108, 116] cm).
Yarn: Bulky-weight blend (42% merino wool, 30% acrylic, 28% superfine alpaca; 109 yd [100 m] per 100 g ball): red marl (yarn A), 6 [6, 7] balls; purple marl (yarn B), 5 [5, 6] balls.
Needles: Size 10½ (6.5 mm); size 11 (8 mm). Adjust needle size if necessary to obtain correct gauge.
Notions: Tapestry needle.
Gauge: 11 sts x 17 rows = 4" (10 cm) in stockinette stitch using size 11 (8 mm) needles.

Abbreviations
k—knit
m1—make 1 stitch by picking up horizontal strand before next stitch with right needle, slipping it onto left needle, and knitting through back of loop
p—purl
skpo—slip 1 stitch, knit 1 stitch, pass slip stitch over
RS—right side
tog—together
WS—wrong side
yo—yarnover

Back

Using size 10½ (6.5 mm) needles and yarn A, cast on 56 [60, 64] sts.
Row 1: (RS) Knit.
Row 2: Purl.
Rows 3–4: Repeat rows 1–2.
Rows 5–6 (hemline): Knit.
Rows 7–10: Repeat rows 1–2 twice.
Change to size 11 (8 mm) needles.
Starting with a knit row, continue working in stockinette stitch using the yarns indicated.
Rows 11–16: Yarn A.
Rows 17–26: Yarn B.
Rows 27–36: Yarn A.
Continue alternating yarns A and B every 10 rows until work measures 14½ [16½, 17]" (37 [42, 43] cm) from hemline, ending with a WS row.
Note: When only one number or set of instructions is given, it applies to all sizes.

Armholes

Continuing to work in stockinette stitch and maintaining the stripe sequence, bind off 3 sts at beginning of next two rows (50 [54, 58] sts).
Continue until armhole measures 8¾ [9, 11]" (22 [23, 28] cm) from beginning of armhole shaping, ending with a WS row.

Shoulders and neck

Continue to work in stockinette stitch, starting with a knit row.
Rows 1–2: Bind off 6 sts at beginning of both rows (38 [42, 46] sts).
Row 3: (RS) Bind off 5 [6, 7] sts knitwise, knit until there are 9 sts on right needle, bind off 10 [12, 14] sts knitwise, knit to end. Work each shoulder separately.
Row 4: Bind off 5 [6, 7] sts purlwise, purl to end.
Row 5: Bind off 4 sts knitwise, knit to end.
Row 6: Bind off remaining 5 sts purlwise.
With WS facing, rejoin yarn to remaining sts at neck edge.
Row 1: Bind off 4 sts purlwise, purl to end.
Row 2: Bind off remaining 5 sts knitwise.

Row 8: Knit.
Row 9: Bind off 6 sts purlwise, purl to end.
Row 10: Knit.
Row 11: Bind off 5 [6, 7] sts purlwise, purl to end.
Row 12: Knit.
Row 13: Bind off remaining 5 sts purlwise.
With WS facing, rejoin yarn to remaining sts at neck edge.
Row 1: P1, p2tog, p18 [19, 20].
Row 2: K17 [18, 19], k2tog, k1.
Row 3: P1, p2tog, p16 [17, 18].
Row 4: K15 [16, 17], k2tog, k1.
Row 5: Purl.
Row 6: K14 [15, 16], k2tog, k1.
Row 7: Purl.
Row 8: Bind off 6 sts knitwise, knit to end.
Row 9: Purl.
Row 10: Bind off 5 [6, 7] sts knitwise, knit to end.
Row 11: Purl.
Row 12: Bind off remaining 5 sts knitwise.

Sleeves

Using size 11 (8 mm) needles and yarn A, cast on 30 [36, 40] sts.
Row 1: Knit.
Row 2: Purl.
Rows 3–4: Repeat rows 1–2 once.
Rows 5–6 (hemline): Knit.
Rows 7–10: Repeat rows 1–2 twice.
Rows 11–12: Working in stockinette stitch and keeping the 10-row stripe repeat in sequence as on back, work two rows.
Increase as follows.
Row 13: K1, m1 knitwise, knit to last 2 sts, m1 knitwise, k1.
Rows 14–18: Work in stockinette stitch, starting with a purl row.
Repeat rows 13–18 until 48 [50, 54] sts are on needle.

Front

Cast on and work rows 1–7 as instructed for the back.
Row 8: P23 [25, 27], p2tog, yo, p6, yo, p2tog, p23 [25, 27].
Rows 9–10: Work as back.
Continue working as for the back until 8 [8, 10] fewer rows have been worked than on the back to the start of the shoulder shaping, ending with a WS row.

Shoulders and neck

Next row: (RS) Knit 21 [22, 23] sts, bind off 8 [10, 12] sts knitwise, knit to end.
Work each shoulder separately.
Row 1: (WS) P18 [19, 20], p2tog tbl, p1.
Row 2: K1, skpo, k17 [18, 19].
Row 3: P16 [17, 18], p2tog tbl, p1.
Row 4: K1, skpo, k15 [16, 17].
Row 5: Purl.
Row 6: K1, skpo, k14 [15, 16].
Row 7: Purl.

Work even in stripes pattern until sleeve measures 16 [17, 17½]" (40 [43, 44] cm) from hemline, ending with a WS row. Bind off loosely. Make second sleeve same.

Left hood

Using yarn A and size 11 (8 mm) needles, cast on 8 [9, 8] sts.

Rows 1–2: Work in stockinette stitch, starting with a knit row.

Row 3: Cast on 3 sts, knit to end (11 [12, 11] sts).

Row 4: Purl.

Rows 5–8: Repeat rows 3–4 twice more (17 [18, 17] sts).

Row 9: Cast on 4 [5, 3] sts, knit to end (21 [23, 20] sts).

Row 10: Purl.

Large size only:

Row 11: Cast on 5 sts, knit to end (25 sts).

Row 12: Purl.

All sizes: Continue straight in stockinette stitch until work measures 12" (30.5 cm) along shortest side, ending with a WS row.

Next row: Skpo, knit to last 2 sts, k2tog (19 [21, 23] sts).

Next row: Purl.

Bind off knitwise.

Right hood

Using yarn A and size 11 (8 mm) needles, cast on 5 [6, 5] sts.

Row 1: Knit.

Row 2: Cast on 3 sts, purl to end (8 [9, 8] sts).

Rows 3–8: Repeat rows 1–2 three more times (17 [18, 17] sts).

Row 9: Knit.

Row 10: Cast on 4 [5, 3] sts, purl to end (21 [23, 20] sts).

Large size only:

Row 11: Knit.

Row 12: Cast on 5 sts, purl to end (25 sts).

All sizes: Complete to match left hood.

Hood edging

Place the left and right hood pieces together and sew the back and top seam using backstitch or mattress stitch. Using yarn A and size 11 (8 mm) needles, and with RS of facing, pick up and knit 83 [83, 85] sts along edge of front opening of hood.

Row 1: Purl.

Row 2: Knit.

Bind off purlwise.

Finishing

With a tapestry needle, weave in the loose yarn tails to WS of work. Join the shoulder seams with backstitch or mattress stitch. Small and medium sizes: Join the sleeve top to armhole, ignoring the 3 sts bind-off at the armhole beginning on back and front. Join the side seams. Join the sleeve seams, sewing top 1" (2.5 cm) of sleeve across 3 sts bind-off. Large size: Join the side and sleeve seams. Ease the sleeve cap into the armhole and stitch. All sizes: Sew the cuffs and hems. Fold along the hemline and turn to the inside. Slip-stitch hem into place. Pin the base of the hood around the neckline of the sweater, centering the hood opening at the center of the front neck. Sew in place using backstitch or mattress stitch. Make a twisted cord tie (see page 49) and thread it through the hem at lower edge of body.

Twisted cord

Twisted cords are a simple way of creating a sturdy drawstring. You can use the same yarn as the rest of the project, or turn it into a design detail by making it in a contrasting color. Twisted cords can be made by twisting together any number of strands; each strand should be about two-and-a-half times the desired finished length of the cord.

1 Measure out the required lengths of yarn and knot each end together. Secure one end to a door handle or similar anchor. Holding the free end of the yarn, stand far enough away from the anchored end so the yarn does not droop. Insert a pencil between the knotted strands in your hand. Twist the pencil and yarn around in one direction until it is tight, and the twisted yarn wants to curl back on itself. It is important at this stage to get plenty of twist into the yarn.

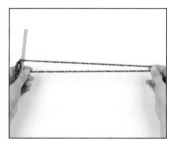

2 Holding the free end firmly in one hand pinch the middle of the yarn with the thumb and forefinger of your other hand. Take the free end up to the secured end and let go of the middle of the yarn. If the cord is too long for you to do this yourself, ask a friend to help.

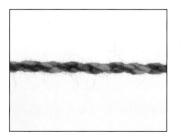

3 The yarn will twist itself into a cord (if it seems too slack, more twisting is needed). Knot the ends together to prevent the cord from untwisting, and smooth out any bumps using your fingers.

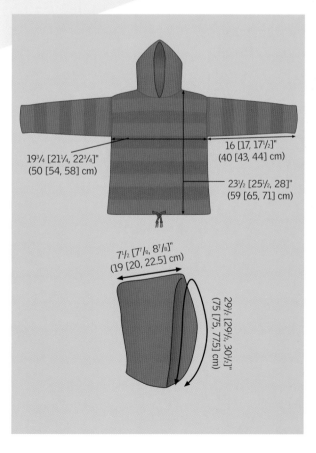

19¾ [21¼, 22¾]" (50 [54, 58] cm)

16 [17, 17½]" (40 [43, 44] cm)

23½ [25½, 28]" (59 [65, 71] cm)

7½ [7⅞, 8⅞]" (19 [20, 22.5] cm)

29½ [29½, 30½]" (75 [75, 77.5] cm)

Textured zip-up top

This textured zip-fronted sweater is worked in an Aran cotton-blend yarn, making it an ideal weight for everyday wear. It is a good project for practicing your basic techniques because it uses a little bit of everything, from reading charts to increasing and decreasing. The zigzag pattern is easily created with basic knit and purl stitches.

THE KNITTY GRITTY

Size: Small [medium, large]; chest (actual): 38 [41½, 45½]" (96.5 [105.5, 115.5] cm).

Yarn: Aran-weight cotton (55% cotton, 45% microfiber; 98 yd [90 m] per 50 g ball): beige, 11 [12, 13] balls.

Needles: Size 6 (4 mm); size 8 (5 mm). Adjust size of needles if necessary to obtain correct gauge.

Notions: Tapestry needle; 24" (61 cm) long open-end zipper; sewing needle and thread.

Gauge: 16 sts x 23 rows = 4" (10 cm) in stockinette stitch using size 8 (5 mm) needles.

Abbreviations

k—knit
k1f&b—knit into front and back of stitch
m1—make 1 stitch by picking up horizontal strand before next stitch with right needle, slipping it onto left needle, and knitting through back of loop
p—purl
RS—right side
skpo—slip 1, knit 1, pass slip stitch over
st(s)—stitch(es)
tog—together
WS—wrong side

Back

Using size 6 (4 mm) needles, cast on 75 [87, 93] sts.
Row 1: (RS) *P3, k3, repeat from * to last 3 [3, 3] sts, p3 [3, 3].
Row 2: *K3, p3, repeat from * to last 3 [3, 3] sts, k3 [3, 3].
Rows 1–2 form the ribbing.
Rows 3–12: Repeat rows 1–2 five more times.
Row 13: Repeat row 1.
Row 14: Small size: K1f&b, rib to last st, k1f&b. Medium size: k2tog, rib to last 2 sts, k2tog. Large size: repeat row 2 (77 [85, 93] sts). Change to size 8 (5 mm) needles.
Rows 15–16: Work in stockinette stitch, starting with a knit row.
Rows 17–47: Work from chart. Continue in stockinette stitch, starting with a purl row, until work measures 13 [13⅜, 13¾]" (33 [34, 35] cm), ending with a WS row.

Chart

Right Front → | ← Left Front

Back

L M S   S M L

Key

Key

☐ k on RS;
p on WS

⊡ p on RS;
k on WS

Armholes

Starting with a knit row, continue in
stockinette stitch and shaping as follows.
Rows 1–2: Bind off 3 [4, 5] sts, work to
end (71 [77, 83] sts).
Row 3: K2, sl 1, k2tog, psso, knit to last
5 sts, k3tog, k2.
Row 4: Purl.
Repeat rows 3–4 one [two, three] times
(63 [65, 67] sts).
Work two rows in stockinette stitch,
starting with a knit row.
 Repeat row 3 (59 [61, 63] sts).
  Work three rows in stockinette stitch,
  starting with a purl row.
  Repeat row 3 (55 [57, 59] sts).
  Continue straight in stockinette
  stitch, starting with a purl row,
  until armhole measures 8 [8¼, 8½]"
  (20.5 [21, 22.5] cm), ending with a
 WS row. Keep a note of how many
rows you work to reach this length.

Shoulders and back neck

Rows 1–2: Bind off 5 sts, work to end
(45 [41, 49] sts).
Row 3: Bind off 5 sts knitwise, knit until
there are 9 sts on right needle, bind off
17 [19, 21] sts knitwise, knit to end.
Work each side separately.

Row 4: Bind off 5 sts purlwise, purl
to end.
Row 5: Bind off 4 sts knitwise, knit
to end.
Row 6: Bind off remaining 5 sts purlwise.
With WS facing, rejoin yarn to remaining
sts at neck edge.
Row 1: Bind off 4 sts purlwise, purl
to end.
Row 2: Bind off remaining 5 sts knitwise.

Left front

Using size 6 (4 mm) needles, cast on
38 [42, 46] sts.
Row 1: (RS) P0 [2, 0], k1 [3, 3], *p3, k3,
repeat from * to last st, p1.
Row 2: K1, *p3, k3, repeat from * to last
1 [5, 3] sts, p1 [3, 3], k0 [2, 0].
Rows 1–2 form the ribbing.
Rows 3–14: Repeat rows 1–2 six
more times.
Change to size 8 (5 mm) needles.
Rows 15–16: Work in stockinette stitch,
starting with a knit row.
Rows 17–47: Work from Left Front chart.
Continue in stockinette stitch, starting
with a purl row, until work matches back
to beginning of armhole shaping, ending
with a WS row.

Armhole

Row 1: (RS) Bind off 3 [4, 5] sts knitwise, knit to end (35 [38, 41] sts).

Row 2: Purl.

Row 3: K2, sl 1, k2tog, psso, knit to end (33 [36, 39] sts).

Row 4: Purl.

Repeat rows 3–4 one [two, three] times (31 [32, 33] sts).

Work two rows in stockinette stitch, starting with a knit row.

Repeat row 3 (29 [30, 31] sts).

Work three rows in stockinette stitch, starting with a purl row.

Repeat row 3 (27 [28, 29] sts).

Continue straight in stockinette stitch, starting with a purl row, until 15 [15, 17] fewer rows have been worked than on back to start of shoulder shaping, ending with a RS row.

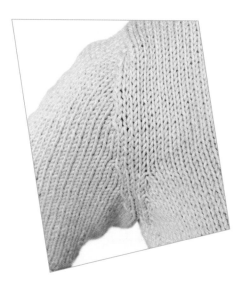

Neck and shoulder

Note: When only one number or set of instructions is given, it applies to all three sizes.

Row 1: (WS) Beginning at neck edge, bind off 4 [5, 6] sts purlwise, purl to end (23 sts).

Row 2: Knit to last 3 sts, k2tog, k1 (22 sts).

Row 3: P1, p2tog, purl to end (21 sts).

Rows 4–5: Repeat rows 2–3 (19 sts).

Row 6: Repeat row 2 (18 sts).

Row 7: Purl.

Rows 8–13: Repeat rows 6–7 three times (15 sts).

Rows 14–15: Work in stockinette stitch.

Large size only: Work two more rows in stockinette stitch.

All sizes: Work the shoulder as follows.

Row 1: (RS) Beginning at armhole edge, bind off 5 sts knitwise, knit to end (10 sts).

Row 2: Purl.

Rows 3–4: Repeat rows 1–2 (5 sts).

Row 5: Bind off remaining 5 sts knitwise.

Right front

Using size 6 (4 mm) needles, cast on 38 [42, 46] sts.

Row 1: (RS) P1, *k3, p3, repeat from * to last 1 [5, 3] sts, k1 [3, 3], p0 [2, 0].

Row 2: K0 [2, 0], p1 [3, 3], *k3, p3, repeat from * to last st, k1.

Rows 1–2 form the ribbing.

Rows 3–14: Repeat rows 1–2 six more times.

Change to size 8 (5 mm) needles.

Rows 15–16: Work in stockinette stitch, starting with a knit row.

Rows 17–47: Work from Right Front chart.

Continue in stockinette stitch, starting with a purl row, until front matches back to beginning of armhole shaping, ending with a RS row.

Armhole

Row 1: (WS) Bind off 3 [4, 5] sts purlwise, purl to end (35 [38, 41] sts).

Row 2: Knit to last 5 sts, k3tog, psso, k2.

Row 3: Purl.

Repeat rows 2–3 one [two, three] times (31 [32, 33] sts).

Work two rows in stockinette stitch, starting with a knit row.

Repeat row 2 (29 [30, 31] sts).

Work three rows in stockinette stitch, starting with a purl row.

Repeat row 2 (27 [28, 29] sts).

Continue straight in stockinette stitch, starting with a purl row, until 14 [14, 16] fewer rows have been worked than on back at start of shoulder shaping, ending with a WS row.

Neck and shoulder

Row 1: (RS) Beginning at neck edge, bind off 4 [5, 6] sts knitwise, knit to end (23 sts).

Row 2: Purl to last 3 sts, p2tog tbl, p1 (22 sts).

Row 3: K1, skpo, knit to end (21 sts).

Rows 4–5: Repeat rows 2–3 (19 sts).

Row 6: Purl.

Row 7: Repeat row 3 (18 sts).

Rows 8–13: Repeat rows 6–7 three times (15 sts).

Row 14: Purl.

Large size only: Work two more rows in stockinette stitch.

All sizes: Work the shoulder as follows.

Row 1: Bind off 5 sts knitwise, knit to end.

Row 2: Purl.

Rows 3–4: Repeat rows 1–2.

Row 5: Bind off remaining 5 sts knitwise.

Sleeves

Using size 6 (4 mm) needles, cast on
43 [45, 47] sts.
Row 1: K2 [3, 1], *p3, k3, repeat from
* to last 5 [6, 4] sts, p3, k2 [3, 1].
Row 2: P2 [3, 1], *k3, p3, repeat from
* to last 5 [6, 4] sts, k3, p2 [3, 1].
Rows 1 and 2 form the ribbing.
Rows 3–14: Repeat rows 1–2 six
more times.
Change to size 8 (5 mm) needles
and stockinette stitch.
***Row 1:** (RS) K3, m1, knit to last 3 sts,
m1, k3.
Work 13 [11, 9] rows in stockinette stitch,
starting with a purl row.*
Repeat * to * two [three, four] times
(49 [53, 57] sts).
**Repeat row 1.
Work 15 [13, 11] rows in stockinette
stitch, starting with a purl row.**
Repeat ** to ** again (53 [57, 61] sts).
Repeat row 1 (55 [59, 63] sts).
Continue straight in stockinette
stitch, starting with a purl row,
until sleeve measures 17 [17½, 17½]"
(43 [44.5, 44.5] cm).

Sleeve cap shaping

Rows 1–2: Bind off 3 [4, 5] sts, work
to end (49 [51, 53] sts).
Rows 3–4: Stockinette stitch.

Row 5: K2, sl 1, k2tog, psso, knit to last
5 sts, k3tog, k2 (45 [47, 49] sts).
Rows 6–8: Stockinette stitch, starting
with a purl row.
Row 9: Repeat row 5 (41 [43, 45] sts).
Rows 10–14: Stockinette stitch, starting
with a purl row.
Row 15: Repeat row 5 (37 [39, 41] sts).
Rows 16–22: Stockinette stitch, starting
with a purl row.
Row 23: Repeat row 5 (33 [35, 37] sts).
Rows 24–26: Stockinette stitch, starting
with a purl row.
Rows 27–30: Repeat rows 23–26
(29 [31, 33] sts).
Row 31: Repeat row 5 (25 [27, 29] sts).
Row 32: Purl.
Rows 33–34: Repeat rows 31–32
(21 [23, 25] sts).
Bind off remaining 21 (23, 25) sts
knitwise.
Make a second sleeve in the same way.

Collar

With a tapestry needle, weave
in the loose yarn tails to WS
of work. Press and block all
the pieces to the required size.
Join both shoulder seams
using backstitch.
With RS facing and using
size 6 (4 mm) needles, pick up

and knit 22 [24, 26] sts up right side of
neck, 25 [27, 29] sts from back neck, and
22 [24, 26] sts down left side of neck
(69 [75, 81] sts).
Row 1: P3, *k3, p3, repeat from * to end.
Row 2: K3, *p3, k3, repeat from * to end.
Repeat these two rows until collar
measures about 4" (10 cm).
Bind off ribwise.

Finishing

With a tapestry needle, weave in the loose
yarn tails to WS of work. Pin and baste
the zipper in place (see page 100), then
stitch using backstitch, following the
knitted stitches as a guideline to allow
you to achieve an even distance between
stitches. Join the side and sleeve seams
using backstitch, then ease the sleeve caps
into the armholes and sew into position.

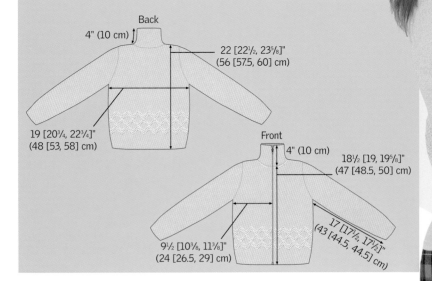

Back
4" (10 cm)
22 [22½, 23⅝]"
(56 [57.5, 60] cm)
19 [20¾, 22¾]"
(48 [53, 58] cm)

Front
4" (10 cm)
18½ [19, 19⅝]"
(47 [48.5, 50] cm)
17 [17¼, 17½]"
(43 [44.5, 44.5] cm)
9½ [10⅜, 11⅜]"
(24 [26.5, 29] cm)

chapter 3

NIGHT OWLS

From simple badges, bangles, and baubles to a shimmering skinny scarf and lacy dress, the projects in this chapter have a party flavor and are ideal for all you clubbers out there. The projects are designed to spark your imagination and encourage you to explore your creative side. So, get edgy with your use of colors and yarns, then go out and flaunt your style.

Distressed hole sweater

Give your sweater that worn and lived in look using simple casting-on and binding-off techniques, along with intentionally dropping stitches. The distressed look is finished off with a lightly felted look. The felting really enhances the holes and leaves the fabric with a soft and cozy brushed effect.

THE KNITTY GRITTY

Size: Chest: 52" (132 cm).
Length: 26" (66 cm)
after felting.
Yarn: Bulky-weight wool
(100% merino wool; approx.
109 yd [100 m] per 100 g
ball): olive, 10 balls.
Needles: Size 10½ (6.5 mm);
size 11 (8 mm). Adjust
needle size if necessary
to obtain correct gauge.
Notions: Stitch holder;
tapestry needle.
Gauge: 11 sts x 16 rows =
4" (10 cm) in stockinette
stitch using size 11 (8 mm)
needles before felting.

Abbreviations
k—knit
k1f&b—knit into front and
back of stitch
p—purl
RS—right side
skpo—slip 1 stitch, knit 1
stitch, pass slip stitch over
tbl—through back of loop
tog—together
WS—wrong side
yo—yarnover

Back

Using size 10½ (6.5 mm) needles, cast on 74 sts.

Row 1: (RS) K2, *p2, k2, repeat from * to end.

Row 2: P2, *k2, p2, repeat from * to end. Rows 1–2 form the ribbing.

Rows 3–12: Repeat rows 1–2 five more times. Change to size 11 (8 mm) needles.

Rows 13–78: Work in stockinette stitch, starting with a knit row.

Armholes

Rows 79–80: Bind off 4 sts, work to end (66 sts).

Row 81: K1, skpo, knit to last 3 sts, k2tog, k1 (64 sts).

Row 82: P1, p2tog, purl to last 3 sts, p2tog tbl, p1 (62 sts).

Row 83: Repeat row 81 (60 sts).

Row 84: Purl.

Rows 85–90: Repeat rows 83–84 three times (54 sts).

Rows 91–118: Work in stockinette stitch, starting with a knit row.

Shoulders and back neck

Continue working in stockinette stitch, starting with a knit row.

Rows 119–120: Bind off 5 sts at beginning of next two rows (44 sts).

Row 121: Bind off 5 sts knitwise, knit until there are 9 sts on the right needle, bind off 16 sts knitwise, knit to end. Work each side of neck separately.

Row 122: At armhole edge, bind off 5 sts purlwise, purl to neck edge.

Row 123: At neck edge, bind off 4 sts knitwise, knit to end of row.

Row 124: Bind off remaining 5 sts purlwise.

With RS facing, rejoin yarn to remaining sts at neck edge.

Row 122: At neck edge, bind off 4 sts purlwise, purl to end of row.

Row 123: At armhole edge, bind off remaining 5 sts knitwise.

Front

Using size 10½ (6.5 mm) needles, cast on 74 sts.

Row 1: (RS) K2, *p2, k2, repeat from * to end.

Row 2: P2, *k2, p2, repeat from * to end. Rows 1–2 form the ribbing.

Rows 3–6: Repeat rows 1–2 twice.

Row 7: Rib 48, bind off 10 sts knitwise, rib to end.

Row 8: Rib 16, cast on 10 sts, rib to end.

Rows 9–10: Repeat rows 1–2.

Row 11: Rib 49, bind off 8 sts knitwise, rib to end.

Row 12: Rib 17, cast on 8 sts, rib to end. Change to size 11 (8 mm) needles and stockinette stitch.

Row 13: Knit.

Row 14: Purl.

Row 15: K49, bind off 6 sts knitwise, knit to end.

Row 16: P19, cast on 6 sts, purl to end.

Rows 17–20: Work in stockinette stitch, starting with a knit row.

Row 21: K16, drop next st, yo, knit to end.

Row 22: P57, p1 tbl, purl to end.

Row 23: Knit.

Row 24: P9, yo, p2tog, purl to end.

Row 25: K36, bind off 3 sts knitwise, knit to end.

Row 26: P35, cast on 3 sts, purl to end.

Row 27: K33, bind off 8 sts knitwise, knit to end.

Row 28: P33, cast on 8 sts, purl to end.

Row 29: Knit.

Row 30: Purl.

Row 31: K32, bind off 10 sts knitwise, knit to end.

Row 32: P32, cast on 10 sts, purl to end.

Row 33: K32, bind off 8 sts knitwise, knit to end.

Row 34: P34, cast on 8 sts, purl to end.

Row 35: K33, bind off 7 sts knitwise, knit to end.

Row 36: P34, cast on 7 sts, purl to end.

Rows 37–38: Repeat rows 35–36.

Row 39: K35, bind off 4 sts knitwise, k25 (includes 1 stitch already on right needle after bind off), drop next st, yo, k9.

Row 40: P35, cast on 4 sts, purl to end.

Row 41: K36, bind off 2 sts knitwise, knit to end.

Row 42: P36, cast on 2 sts, purl to end.

Rows 43–47: Work in stockinette stitch, starting with a knit row.

Row 48: P52, bind off 4 sts purlwise, purl to end.

Row 49: K18, cast on 4 sts, knit to end.

Rows 50–51: Work in stockinette stitch, starting with a purl row.

Row 52: P53, bind off 3 sts purlwise, purl to end.

Row 53: K18, cast on 3 sts, knit to end.

Rows 54–57: Work in stockinette stitch, starting with a purl row.

Row 58: P22, yo, p2tog, purl to end.

Row 59: Knit.

Row 60: Purl.

Row 61: K56, yo, skpo, knit to end.

Rows 62–67: Work in stockinette stitch, starting with a purl row.

Row 68: P22, drop next st, yo, purl to end.

Row 69: K51, k1 tbl, knit to end.

Rows 70–75: Work in stockinette stitch, starting with a purl row.

Row 76: P17, drop next st, yo, purl to end.

Row 77: K56, k1 tbl, knit to end.

Row 78: Purl.

Armholes

Rows 79–80: Bind off 4 sts, work to end (66 sts).

Row 81: K1, skpo, k11, drop next st, yo, knit to last 3 sts, k2tog, k1 (64 sts).

Row 82: P1, p2tog, p47, p1 tbl, p10, p2tog tbl, p1 (62 sts).

Row 83: Repeat row 81 (60 sts).

Row 84: Purl.

Rows 85–90: Repeat rows 83–84 three times (54 sts).

Rows 91–108: Work in stockinette stitch, starting with a knit row.

Row 109: K22, bind off 10 sts knitwise, knit to end.

Shoulders and front neck

Work each side of neck separately.

Row 110: Beginning at armhole edge, purl to last 3 sts at neck edge, p2tog tbl, p1 (21 sts).

Row 111: Beginning at neck edge, k1, skpo, knit to end (20 sts).

Rows 112–115: Repeat rows 110–111 twice (16 sts).

Row 116: Purl.

Row 117: Repeat row 111 (15 sts).

Row 118: Knit.

Row 119: Purl.

Row 120: At armhole edge, bind off 5 sts purlwise, purl to end (10 sts).

Row 121: Knit.

Rows 122–123: Repeat rows 120–121 (5 sts).

Bind off remaining 5 sts purlwise. Rejoin yarn to remaining sts at neck edge.

Row 110: P1, p2tog, purl to end (21 sts).

Row 111: K1, knit to last 3 sts, k2tog, k1 (20 sts).

Rows 112–115: Repeat rows 110–111 twice (16 sts).

Row 116: Purl.

Row 117: Repeat row 111 (15 sts).

Row 118: Purl.

Row 119: Bind off 5 sts knitwise, knit to end (10 sts).

Row 120: Purl.

Rows 121–122: Repeat rows 119–120 (5 sts).

Row 123: Bind off remaining 5 sts knitwise.

Left sleeve

Using size 10½ (6.5 mm) needles, cast on 40 sts.

Row 1: (RS) K1, p2, *k2, p2, repeat from * to last st, k1.

Row 2: P1, k2, *p2, k2, repeat from * to last st, p1.

Rows 1 and 2 form the ribbing.

Rows 3–12: Repeat rows 1–2 five more times.

Change to size 11 (8 mm) needles and stockinette stitch, starting with a knit row.

Row 13: K1f&b, knit to last st, k1f&b (42 sts).

Rows 14–20: Work in stockinette stitch, starting with a purl row.

Rows 21–36: Repeat rows 13–20 twice (46 sts).

Row 37: Repeat row 13 (48 sts).

Rows 38–46: Work in stockinette stitch, starting with a purl row.

Rows 47–66: Repeat rows 37–46 twice (52 sts).

Row 67: Repeat row 13 (54 sts).

Rows 68–80: Work in stockinette stitch, starting with a purl row.

Sleeve cap shaping

Rows 81–82: Bind off 4 sts, work to end (46 sts).

Row 83: K1, skpo, knit to last 3 sts, k2tog, k1 (44 sts).

Row 84: P1, p2tog, purl to last 3 sts, p2tog tbl, p1 (42 sts).

Row 85: Repeat row 83 (40 sts).

Row 86: Purl.

Row 87: Repeat row 83 (38 sts).

Rows 88–90: Work in stockinette stitch, starting with a purl row.

Rows 91–98: Repeat rows 87–90 twice (34 sts).

Row 99: Repeat row 83 (32 sts).

Row 100: Purl.

Rows 101–104: Repeat rows 83–84 twice (24 sts).

Row 105: Bind off knitwise.

Right sleeve

Rows 1–12: Cast on 40 sts and work in rib as for left sleeve.

Change to size 11 (8 mm) needles.

Row 13: (RS) K1f&b, k30, yo, skpo, k6, k1f&b (42 sts).

Rows 14–18: Work in stockinette stitch, starting with a purl row.

Row 19: K11, drop next st, yo, knit to end.

Row 20: P30, p1 tbl, purl to end.

Row 21: K1f&b, knit to last st, k1f&b (44 sts).

Rows 22–25: Work in stockinette stitch, starting with a purl row.

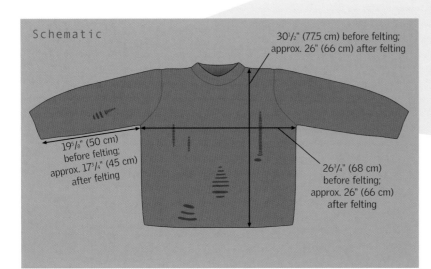

Schematic

30½" (77.5 cm) before felting; approx. 26" (66 cm) after felting

19⅝" (50 cm) before felting; approx. 17¾" (45 cm) after felting

26¾" (68 cm) before felting; approx. 26" (66 cm) after felting

Row 26: P10, drop next st, yo, purl to end.
Row 27: K33, k1 tbl, k10.
Row 28: Purl.
Row 29: Repeat row 21 (46 sts).
Rows 30–36: Work in stockinette stitch, starting with a purl row.
Row 37: K1f&b, k23, bind off 12 sts knitwise, knit to last st, k1f&b.
Row 38: P11, cast on 12 sts, purl to end (48 sts).
Row 39: K30, bind off 5 sts knitwise, knit to end.
Row 40: P13, cast on 5 sts, purl to end.
Row 41: K31, bind off 3 sts knitwise, knit to end.
Row 42: P14, cast on 3 sts, purl to end.
Rows 43–46: Work in stockinette stitch, starting with a knit row.
Row 47: Repeat row 21 (50 sts).
Row 48: Purl.
Row 49: Knit.
Row 50: P10, bind off 4 sts purlwise, purl to end.
Row 51: K36, cast on 4 sts, knit to end.
Row 52: Purl.
Row 53: K10, bind off 4 sts knitwise, knit to end.
Row 54: P36, cast on 4 sts, purl to end.
Row 55: Knit.
Row 56: Purl.
Row 57: Repeat row 21 (52 sts).
Row 58: Purl.
Row 59: Knit.
Row 60: P38, drop next st, yo, purl to end.
Row 61: K14, k1 tbl, knit to end.
Rows 62–66: Work in stockinette stitch, starting with a purl row.
Row 67: Repeat row 21 (54 sts).
Rows 68–105: Work as for left sleeve.

Collar

With a tapestry needle, weave in the loose yarn tails on front and back pieces to WS of work. Join the right shoulder seam using backstitch or mattress stitch. With RS facing and using size 10½ (6.5 mm) needles, pick up and knit 14 sts down left side of neck, 10 sts across front neck, 14 sts up right side of neck, then 24 sts from back neck (62 sts in total).
Row 1: (WS) P2, *k2, p2, repeat from * to end.
Row 2: K2, *p2, k2 repeat from * to end.
Rows 3–10: Repeat rows 1–2 four more times.
Change to size 11 (8 mm) needles.
Bind off loosely in ribbing.

Finishing

With a tapestry needle, join the left shoulder seam and neckband, then join the side and sleeve seams, using backstitch or mattress stitch. Ease the sleeve caps into the armholes and sew into place. Lightly felt the sweater so that stitch definition remains visible (see page 81).

Extra-long skinny scarf

Knitted in bright cotton and shiny lurex yarns to create flashes of vibrant color, both boys and girls will look funky in this extremely long skinny scarf. Just vary the colors to suit your taste, then keep wrapping it around and around. Knitted in garter stitch, this is a really easy scarf to make, but it is knitted lengthwise to give vertical rather than horizontal stripes, making it look even longer and skinnier.

THE KNITTY GRITTY

Size: 3" (7.5 cm) wide x 120" (300 cm) long.

Yarn: Medium-weight cotton (100% cotton; 125 yd [115 m] per 50 g ball): pink (yarn A), 2 balls; red (yarn B), 1 ball. Light-weight lurex (80% viscose, 20% polyester; 104 yd [95 m] per 25 g ball): purple (yarn C), 1 ball.

Needles: Size 5 (3.75 mm) circular, 40" (101.5 cm) or longer.

Gauge: 11 sts x 20 rows = 2" (5 cm) in garter stitch with yarns A, B, and C using size 5 (3.75 mm) needles. Exact gauge isn't necessary.

Abbreviations
st(s)—stitch(es)

Note
The scarf is worked in garter stitch, and is worked back and forth as if using two needles. However, you will need to use a long circular needle because of the number of stitches. The pattern does not require that you work in the round.

Garter stripes

Cast on 650 sts using a long size 5 (3.75 mm) circular needle and yarn A. Follow the stripe sequence listed below, carrying the yarns up the side of the work when not in use (see page 45).

Rows 1–2: Yarn A.
Rows 3–4: Yarn C.
Rows 5–6: Yarn A.
Rows 7–8: Yarn B.
Rows 9–10: Yarn C.
Rows 11–12: Yarn B.
Rows 13–14: Yarn A.
Rows 15–16: Yarn C.
Rows 17–18: Yarn A.
Rows 19–20: Yarn B.
Rows 21–22: Yarn C.
Rows 23–24: Yarn B (cut yarn B after row 24).
Rows 25–26: Yarn A.
Rows 27–28: Yarn C (cut yarn C after row 28).
Rows 29–30: Yarn A.
Bind off loosely purlwise.

Finishing

With a tapestry needle, weave in the loose yarn tails to one side of the work and secure. Gently block and press to the required length if necessary.

Fingerless gloves

These gloves are knitted using a twisting cable design, producing a rich vertical texture to complement the horizontal stripe pattern. There are no separate finger pieces, making them much easier to knit than normal gloves, and the thumb is worked in stockinette stitch rather than cable to make things simpler still. Refer to page 45 for guidance on carrying multiple yarns up the side of the work.

THE KNITTY GRITTY

Size: To fit average-sized adult's hands. Length: 7⅝" (19.5 cm). Circumference around widest part of hand: 5½" (14 cm).
Yarn: DK-weight blend (50% merino wool, 50% cotton; 123 yd [113 m] per 50 g ball): green (yarn A), 1 ball; cream (yarn B), 1 ball.
Needles: Size 3 (3.25 mm); size 5 (3.75 mm). Adjust needle size if necessary to obtain correct gauge.
Notions: Tapestry needle.
Gauge: 24 sts x 32 rows = 4" (10 cm) in stockinette stitch using size 5 (3.75 mm) needles.

Abbreviations
2/2RC—right-cross cable; see step-by-step sequence on page 63
k—knit
m1—make 1 stitch by picking up horizontal strand before next stitch with right needle, slipping it onto left needle, and knitting through back of loop
p—purl
RS—right side
st(s)—stitch(es)

Wrist section

Using size 3 (3.25 mm) needles and yarn A, cast on 50 sts.
Row 1: (RS) (K2, p2, k4, p2) twice, (k2, p2) twice, (k2, p2, k4, p2) twice, k2.
Row 2: (P2, k2, p4, k2) twice, (p2, k2) twice, (p2, k2, p4, k2) twice, p2.
Row 3: (K2, p2, 2/2RC, p2) twice, (k2, p2) twice, (k2, p2, 2/2RC p2) twice, k2.
Row 4: Repeat row 2.

Rows 1–4 form the cable pattern repeat.
Rows 5–16: Join yarn B and work the above pattern repeat three more times, alternating four rows using yarn B, four rows using yarn A, and 4 rows using yarn B (12 rows).
Rows 17–32: Change to size 5 (3.75 mm) needles and continue the pattern repeat four more times, again alternating yarns A and B every four rows.

Thumb gusset

The thumb and gusset are worked in stockinette stitch, while the hand part of the glove continues in the cable pattern.
Row 33: (RS) (K2, p2, k4, p2) twice, k2, p2, m1, k2, m1, p2, (k2, p2, k4, p2) twice, k2 (52 sts).
Row 34: (P2, k2, p4, k2) five times, p2.
Row 35: (K2, p2, 2/2RC, p2) twice, k2, p2, m1, k4, m1, p2, (k2, p2, 2/2RC, p2) twice, k2 (54 sts).
Row 36: (P2, k2, p4, k2) twice, p2, k2, p6, k2, (p2, k2, p4, k2) twice, p2.
Row 37: (K2, p2, k4, p2) twice, k2, p2, m1, k6, m1, p2, (k2, p2, k4, p2) twice, k2 (56 sts).
Row 38: (P2, k2, p4, k2) twice, p2, k2, p8, k2, (p2, k2, p4, k2) twice, p2.
Row 39: (K2, p2, 2/2RC, p2) twice, k2, p2, m1, k8, m1, p2, (k2, p2, 2/2RC, p2) twice, k2 (58 sts).
Row 40: (P2, k2, p4, k2) twice, p2, k2, m1, p10, m1, k2, (p2, k2, p4, k2) twice, p2 (60 sts).

Right-cross cable (2/2RC)

The cable pattern on the gloves crosses two stitches to the right.

1 Slip two stitches from the left needle onto a cable needle and hold the cable needle at the back of the work. Knit the next two stitches from the left needle.

2 Bring the cable needle into knitting position and knit the two stitches. You have now completed a 2/2 right-cross cable.

Thumb

Next row: (RS) (K2, p2, k4, p2) twice, k2, p2, k12, turn, leaving remaining stitches unworked until later.
Next row: P12, turn.
Next row: Cast on 2 sts at beginning of row, k14, turn (14 sts). Starting with a purl row, work nine rows in stockinette stitch on these 14 sts. Bind off purlwise. Cut yarn, leaving a tail long enough to sew the thumb seam. Thread a tapestry needle with the long yarn tail and sew the thumb seam using backstitch or mattress stitch.

Hand

With RS facing, pick up and knit 2 sts from the base of the thumb, then using the remaining stitches on left needle (these are the unworked stitches from the first thumb row), p2, (k2, p2, k4, p2) twice, k2 (26 sts on left side of thumb, 24 stitches on right—50 sts).

Using all 50 stitches, work another 17 rows in cable pattern—that is, repeat rows 1–4, starting and ending with row 2.
Bind off in pattern.

To finish

With a tapestry needle, weave in the loose yarn tails to WS of work and sew the side seam using backstitch or mattress stitch. Repeat to make a second glove.

Arty badges

Even the dullest outfit can be jazzed up with these easy-to-knit felted badges. They are really quick to make so you can knit lots of them in a variety of colors to mix and match with different outfits, and they are an ideal way to use up scraps of yarn. The way you decorate them is entirely up to you, so they are a great way to express your individual sense of style.

THE KNITTY GRITTY

Size: Large badge: about 4" (10 cm) diameter. Small badge: about 3" (7.5 cm) diameter.
Yarn: Scraps of bulky-weight wool (100% pure new wool): red (yarn A). Scraps of DK-weight wool (100% pure new wool): green (yarn B); blue (yarn C). Note: Don't use superwash wools or synthetic yarns because these yarns will not felt.
Needles: Size 8 (5 mm); size 17 (12 mm).
Notions: Tapestry needle; glass beads; sequins; two pin backs, available from craft stores or online jewelry suppliers; sewing thread and needle for attaching decoration and pin backs. Note: Size and shape of sequins and beads are not important. Choose decorations that best suit your finished badge.
Gauge: Not important.

Abbreviations
k1f&b—knit into front and back of stitch
p—purl
p1f&b—purl into front and back of stitch
st(s)—stitch(es)
WS—wrong side

Large badge
Using size 17 (12 mm) needles and yarn A, cast on 8 sts.
Row 1: (WS) Purl.
Row 2: K1f&b in every st (16 sts).
Row 3: Purl.
Row 4: Repeat row 2 (32 sts). Bind off knitwise.

Small badge
Using size 8 (5 mm) needles and yarn B, cast on 8 sts.
Row 1: (WS) Purl.
Row 2: K1f&b in every st (16 sts).
Change to yarn C.
Row 3: Purl.
Row 4: Repeat row 2 (32 sts). Change to yarn B.
Row 5: Purl.
Row 6: Knit.
Change to yarn C.
Row 7: *P1b&f in next st, p1, repeat from * to end (48 sts).
Row 8: Knit.
Change to yarn B.
Row 9: Purl.
Bind off purlwise. As you bind off, the work will begin curl around and form a circle.

Sewing on sequins and beads

Adding sequins and beads is a great way to jazz up any knitted piece. They can be sewn to cover an item, or used as an effective design detail, such as a trim or motif. Any size of sequin or bead can be used, but make sure that the needle and thread will pass through the central hole. It is also important that the bead is not too heavy for the yarn you are using, or it will fall forward and pull the fabric.

1 Thread a sharp sewing needle with sewing cotton and anchor the thread into position at the back of the work, either using a backstitch or by tying a knot.

2 Push the needle and thread through to the right side of the fabric, making sure it is in the correct position. Place the bead or sequin on the needle and pull it down the thread toward the fabric.

3 Push the needle back through to the wrong side of the work, making sure that the bead or sequin is firmly attached to the right side. Fasten off securely at the back of the work with a couple of small backstitches.

Finishing

Cut a 12" (30.5-cm) strand of one of the wool yarns, thread the tapestry needle and neatly whipstitch the short sides together, including the cast-on edge in the center to close the circle. With a tapestry needle, weave in the loose yarn tails to WS of work. Felt the badges (see page 81). With a sewing thread and needle, sew sequins onto the small badge and glass beads onto the large badge. Sew a pin back to the back of each badge.

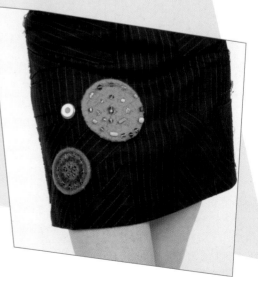

Party dress

This little black dress is knitted in bulky-weight cotton, giving it a beautiful drape. The hem edge and armholes are trimmed with a simple but pretty lace edging, adding that extra special something. This versatile garment can be worn on its own or over the top of jeans for a more casual look.

THE KNITTY GRITTY

Size: Small [medium, large] to fit 34 [36, 38]" (86 [91, 97] cm) bust; 28 [28⅜, 28¾]" (71 [72, 73] cm) length.

Yarn: Bulky-weight cotton (100% cotton; 63 yd [58 m] per 50 g ball): black (yarn A), 12 balls. Medium-weight cotton (100% cotton; 123 yd [113 m] per 50 g ball): black (yarn B), 1 ball.

Needles: Size 6 (4 mm); size 10 (6 mm); size 11 (8 mm). Adjust needle size if necessary to obtain correct gauge.

Notions: Tapestry needle.

Gauge: 12 sts x 17 rows = 4" (10 cm) in stockinette stitch using size 11 (8 mm) needles.

Abbreviations
k—knit
kp (in lace trim pattern)—
see step-by-step sequence on page 69
m1—make 1 stitch by picking up horizontal strand before next stitch with right needle, slipping it onto left needle, and knitting through back of loop
p—purl
RS—right side
skpo—slip 1 stitch, knit 1 stitch, pass slip stitch over
sl 1—slip 1 stitch
st(s)—stitch(es)
tbl—through back of loop
tog—together
WS—wrong side
yo—yarnover

Back

Using size 10 (6 mm) needles and yarn A, cast on 62 [66, 70] sts.
Row 1: (RS) Knit.
Row 2: (WS) Purl.
Rows 3–6: Repeat rows 1–2 twice more. Change to size 11 (8 mm) needles.
Rows 7–26: Starting with a RS row, work 20 rows in stockinette stitch, ending with a WS row.
Row 27: K2, skpo, knit to last 4 sts, k2tog, k2 (60 [64, 68] sts).
Rows 28–30: Work in stockinette stitch, starting with a WS row.
Rows 31–46: Repeat rows 27–30 four times (52 [56, 60] sts).
Row 47: Repeat row 27 (50 [54, 58] sts).
Rows 48–54: Work in stockinette stitch, starting with a WS row.
Row 55: K2, m1 knitwise, knit to last 2 sts, m1 knitwise, k2 (52 [56, 60] sts).
Rows 56–67: Repeat rows 48–55 twice (56 [60, 64] sts). Continue in stockinette stitch, starting with a WS row, until back measures 19½ [20, 20½]" (50 [51, 52] cm), ending with a WS row. Keep a note of how many rows you work to reach this length.

Armholes

With RS facing, continue working in stockinette stitch, starting with a knit row.
Rows 1–2: Bind off 4 sts, work to end of row (48 [52, 56] sts).
Small size only:
Row 3: K1, skpo, knit to last 3 sts, k2tog, k1 (46 sts).
Row 4: Purl.
Rows 5–6: Repeat rows 3–4 (44 sts).
Row 7: Knit.
Row 8: Purl.
Row 9: Repeat row 3 (42 sts).
Medium size only:
Row 3: K1, skpo, knit to last 3 sts, k2tog, k1 (50 sts).

Row 4: P1, p2tog, purl to last 3 sts, p2tog tbl, p1 (48 sts).
Row 5: Repeat row 3 (46 sts).
Row 6: Purl.
Row 7: Knit.
Row 8: Purl.
Row 9: Repeat row 3 (44 sts).
Large size only:
Rows 3–6: Work as for medium size (50 sts).
Row 7: Repeat row 3 (48 sts).
Rows 8–9: Repeat rows 6–7 (46 sts).
Rows 10–12: Work in stockinette stitch, starting with a WS row.
Row 13: Repeat row 3 (44 sts).
All sizes: Continue in stockinette stitch, starting with a WS row, until armhole measures 7 [7, 7½]" (18 [18, 19] cm), ending with a WS row. Keep a note of how many rows you work to reach this length.

Shoulders and back neck

Next row: (RS) Bind off 3 sts knitwise, knit until there are 6 sts on right needle, bind off 24 [26, 26] sts knitwise, knit to end.
Work each side of neck separately.
Row 1: At armhole edge, bind off 3 sts purlwise, purl to neck edge.
Row 2: At neck edge, bind off 3 sts knitwise, knit to end.
Row 3: Bind off remaining 3 sts purlwise.
With WS facing, rejoin yarn to remaining sts at neck edge.
Row 1: (WS) At neck edge, bind off 3 sts purlwise, purl to end.
Row 2: At armhole edge, bind off remaining 3 sts knitwise.

Front

Work as instructed for the back until eight fewer rows have been worked than on the back to beginning of shoulder shaping, ending with a WS row (42 [44, 44] sts).

Front neck and shoulders

Next row: (RS) K11, bind off 20 [22, 22] sts knitwise, knit to end.

Work each side of the neck separately.

Row 1: P8, p2tog tbl, p1 (10 sts).

Row 2: K1, skpo, k7 (9 sts).

Row 3: P6, p2tog tbl, p1 (8 sts).

Row 4: Knit.

Row 5: P5, p2tog tbl, p1 (7 sts).

Row 6: Knit.

Row 7: P4, p2tog tbl, p1 (6 sts).

Row 8: Knit.

Row 9: Bind off 3 sts purlwise, purl to end.

Row 10: Knit.

Row 11: Bind off remaining 3 sts purlwise.

With WS facing, rejoin yarn to remaining sts at neck edge and work as follows.

Row 1: P1, p2tog, p8 (10 sts).

Row 2: K7, k2tog, k1 (9 sts).

Row 3: P1, p2tog, p6 (8 sts).

Row 4: Knit.

Row 5: P1, p2tog, p5 (7 sts).

Row 6: Knit.

Row 7: P1, p2tog, p4 (6 sts).

Row 8: Bind off 3 sts knitwise, knit to end.

Row 9: Purl.

Row 10: Bind off remaining 3 sts knitwise.

Neckband

Block and press both pieces to the required size. With a tapestry needle, sew the right shoulder seam using backstitch or mattress stitch. With RS facing and using size 10 (6 mm) needles, begin at front left shoulder, pick up and knit 8 sts down left side of front neck, 20 [22, 22] sts across center front, 8 sts up right side of neck, then 32 [34, 34] across back neck (68 [72, 72] sts). Beginning with WS row, knit two rows, then bind off knitwise on WS.

Sew the left shoulder seam and neckband, then the side seams. Weave in the loose yarn tails to WS of work.

Hem lace trim

Using size 11 (8 mm) needles and yarn A, cast on 10 sts.
Row 1: (RS) Sl 1, k2, yo, k2tog, *yo twice, k2tog, repeat from * once, k1 (12 sts).
Row 2: K2, kp, k1, kp, k2, yo, k2tog, k1.
Row 3: Sl 1, k2, yo, k2tog, k2, *yo twice, k2tog, repeat from * once, k1 (14 sts).
Row 4: K2, kp, k1, kp, k4, yo, k2tog, k1.

Row 5: Sl 1, k2, yo, k2tog, k4, *yo twice, k2tog, repeat from * once, k1 (16 sts).
Row 6: K2, kp, k1, kp, k6, yo, k2tog, k1.
Row 7: Sl 1, k2, yo, k2tog, k11.
Row 8: Bind off 6 sts knitwise, k6 (not including st already on needle after binding off), yo, k2tog, k1 (10 sts).
Rows 1–8 form the lace pattern.
Rows 9–192: Repeat rows 1–8 another 23 times.

Armhole lace trim

Using size 6 (4 mm) needles and yarn B, work as instructed for the hem lace trim until the required length is achieved to cover around entire armhole edge. Make a second armhole lace trim in the same way.

Finishing

With RS of lace and garment facing together, and WS facing upward, pin neckline lace trim in place around neckline and armhole trim around armholes. With a tapestry needle and matching yarn, on WS of work, sew the lace trims into position using backstitch. Sew trim side edges together. Using damp press cloth, press lace away from garment.

Lace trim pattern—kp

The knitted lacework trims on this dress may look very complicated, but are actually very easy to do.

1 Work row 1 of the lace trim pattern, wrapping the yarn over the needle twice where indicated.

2 When working row 2 of the pattern, knit into the first yarnover.

3 Then purl into the second yarnover.

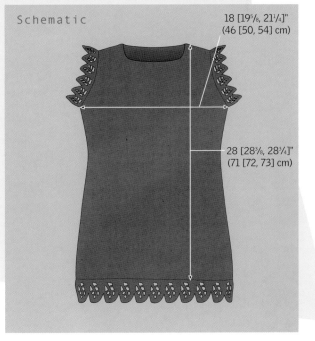

Schematic

18 [19⅝, 21¼]"
(46 [50, 54] cm)

28 [28⅜, 28¾]"
(71 [72, 73] cm)

Bangles and baubles

Create your own knitted jewelry using the simplest of techniques. These beaded necklaces and bangles can easily be made in an evening, and will certainly make you stand out from the crowd. Knitted in bulky and super bulky yarns, the felting process gives them character and structure. Add decorative beads, sequins, and embroidery to jazz them up even more—let your imagination go wild.

THE KNITTY GRITTY

Size: Basic bangle: about 1–2" (2.5–5 cm) wide x 4" (10 cm) diameter. Hole bangle: about 1" (2.5 cm) wide x 3" (7.5 cm) diameter. Large necklace bead: about 2" (5 cm) diameter. Small necklace bead: about 1⅜" (3.5 cm) diameter. Note: Exact measurements will vary due to the felting process.

Yarn: Scraps of bulky- and super bulky-weight wool (100% merino wool). Note: Don't use superwash wools or synthetic yarns because these yarns will not felt.

Needles: Size 17 (12 mm); size 19 (15 mm); size 36 (20 mm).

Notions: Tapestry needle; about 2–3 dozen 8 mm sequins and/or 3 mm glass beads—the actual number of sequins and beads will vary according to how you choose to decorate them; sewing needle and thread for adding decoration; embroidery thread; length of extra thick cotton thread; about 36" (91.5 cm) leather thonging, 2 mm diameter.

Gauge: Not important.

Abbreviations
k—knit
 k1f&b—knit into front and back of stitch
RS—right side
st(s)—stitch(es)
 tog—together
yo—yarnover

Basic bangle

Using size 36 (20 mm) needles and super bulky yarn, cast on 20 sts.
Row 1: (RS) Knit.
Row 2: Purl.
If you want to make the bangle wider, repeat rows 1–2 once more (the white bangle pictured here was knitted with just two rows, the pink sequined bangle with four rows).
Bind off knitwise.

Hole bangle

Using size 17 (12 mm) needles and bulky yarn, cast on 4 sts.
Row 1: (RS) Knit.
Row 2: Purl.
Row 3: K2tog, yo twice, k2tog (4 sts).
Row 4: P1, (p1, k1) into yarnovers of previous row, p1 (4 sts).
Rows 5–16: Repeat rows 3–4 six times.
Bind off knitwise.

Finishing

With a tapestry needle, weave in the loose yarn tails to WS of work and sew the short edges together to form a ring. Felt the bangles (see page 81). A variety of techniques can be used to personalize the basic bangle. For example, add sparkle by sewing sequins and beads around the center. Embroidery works extremely well on felted fabric, so try using blanket stitch (see page 121) in a tonal color to emphasize the holes of the other bangle.

Small necklace bead

Using size 17 (12 mm) needles and bulky yarn, cast on 3 sts.
Row 1: (RS) K1, (k1, p1, k1, p1, k1, p1) in next stitch, k1 (8 sts).
Row 2: Purl.
Row 3: Knit.
Row 4: Purl.
Row 5: K2tog four times (4 sts).
Break off the yarn, draw the tail through the loops on the needle, and fasten off.

Large necklace bead

Using size 36 (20 mm) needles and super bulky yarn, work as instructed for the small bead.

Finishing

With a tapestry needle, weave in the loose yarn tails to WS of work and sew the short edges of the beads together, leaving an opening big enough to insert stuffing.

Make the stuffing by cutting scraps of bulky and super bulky yarn into small pieces. Stuff these into the beads until you achieve a full, rounded shape. Finish sewing the beads. Push a large tapestry needle with a length of thick cotton through the center of the beads to make a hole. Leaving the cotton in place, felt the beads. After felting, you can decorate them with sequins or other embellishments if you wish. Remove the cotton and thread the required number and size of beads onto a length of leather thonging, making sure that you allow enough length to tie the ends together when wearing the necklace.

chapter 4

HOME COMFORTS

With all the stresses of modern-day life, it is extremely satisfying to create knitted pieces for your own home. Turn your home into the perfect comfort zone by cuddling up in the softly cabled snuggle blanket, and keep your toes warm with the cozy felted merino wool slippers. The smaller projects, such as the no-maintenance pot plants and the quirky fruit protectors, are great for using up scraps of yarn.

Fruit protectors

Have you ever discovered at lunchtime that your fruit is covered in cuts and bruises from being jostled around in your lunchbox? How about knitting some fruit protectors? Not only are these pieces functional, but they are also extremely pretty and fun. Knitted in four separate pieces, these fruit protectors use basic stockinette stitch, a few simple increasing and decreasing techniques, then are sewn together and finished off with a button fastening.

THE KNITTY GRITTY

Size: To fit average-sized apple and banana.

Yarn: DK-weight cotton (100% cotton; 93 yd [85 m] per 50 g ball): red or green (apple), 1 ball; yellow (banana), 1 ball. Small amounts of scrap DK yarn in green for apple leaf, and brown for ends of banana.

Needles: Size 6 (4 mm).

Notions: Three ⅝" (15 mm) buttons (one for the apple cover, and two for the banana); tapestry needle; sewing needle and matching color sewing thread to attach buttons if holes are too small to use yarn.

Gauge: 18 sts x 28 rows = 4" (10 cm) in stockinette stitch using size 6 (4 mm) needles. Exact gauge isn't necessary.

Abbreviations
k—knit
k1f&b—knit into front and back of stitch
p—purl
psso—pass slip stitch over
RS—right side
sl 1—slip 1 stitch
tog—together
WS—wrong side

Apple protector

Using size 6 (4 mm) needles and the main color yarn for apple, cast on 4 sts.
Row 1: (RS) Knit.
Row 2: Purl.
Row 3: K1f&b, knit to last stitch, k1f&b (6 sts).
Row 4: Purl.
Row 5: Repeat row 3 (8 sts).
Row 6: Purl.
Row 7: Repeat row 3 (10 sts).
Row 8: Purl.
Row 9: Repeat row 3 (12 sts).
Row 10: Purl.
Row 11: Repeat row 3 (14 sts).
Row 12: Purl.
Row 13: Knit.
Row 14: Purl.
Row 15: K2tog, knit to last 2 sts, k2tog (12 sts).
Row 16: Purl.
Row 17: Repeat row 15 (10 sts).
Row 18: Purl.
Row 19: Repeat row 15 (8 sts).
Row 20: Purl.

Row 21: Repeat row 15 (6 sts).
Row 22: Purl.
Row 23: Repeat row 15 (4 sts).
Row 24: Purl.
Bind off purlwise. Cut yarn, leaving a 4" (10 cm) tail. Make three more pieces in the same way.

Leaf

Using size 6 (4 mm) needles and a few scrap yards (meters) of green yarn, cast on 3 sts.
Row 1: (RS) Knit.
Row 2: Purl.
Row 3: K1f&b, k1, k1f&b (5 sts).
Row 4: Purl.
Row 5: K2tog, k1, k2tog (3 sts).
Row 6: Purl.
Row 7: Sl 1, k2tog, psso. Fasten off the end of yarn. Cut yarn, leaving a 4" (10 cm) tail.

Finishing

With a tapestry needle, weave in the loose yarn tails to WS of work. Sew three of the apple pieces together along the whole seams using backstitch or mattress stitch, then sew the fourth piece in place, but only sew half the length of the seam in order to create an opening for the fruit. Sew a small button to one side of this opening. On the opposite side, attach yarn and make a loop just large enough to close around the button. Sew the leaf to the top of the apple protector on the opposite side of the fastening, with the right side of the leaf uppermost (see photo).

Banana

Using size 6 (4 mm) needles and a few scrap yards (meters) of brown yarn, cast on 4 sts.
Row 1: (RS) Knit.
Row 2: Purl.
Cut the brown yarn, leaving a 4" (10 cm) tail, and join the main color.
Row 3: K1f&b, knit to last stitch, k1f&b (6 sts).
Row 4: Purl.
Row 5: Repeat row 3 (8 sts).
Row 6: Purl.

Row 7: Repeat row 3 (10 sts). Starting with a purl row, continue in stockinette stitch until work measures 8" (20.5 cm), ending with a WS row. You can adjust the size of the banana protector by working more or fewer rows of stockinette stitch before starting the decreases.
Decrease row: (RS) K2tog, knit to last 2 stitches, k2tog (8 sts).
Next row: Purl.
Next row: Repeat decrease row (6 sts).
Break off the main color yarn and join the brown yarn again.
Next row: Purl.
Next row: Repeat decrease row (4 sts).
Next row: P1, p2tog, p1 (3 sts).

Starting with a knit row, work four more rows in stockinette stitch. Bind off purlwise. Make three more pieces in the same way, but make one of them measuring only 7½" (19 cm) long for the shorter inside edge of the banana.

Finishing

With a tapestry needle, weave in the loose yarn tails to WS of work. Sew the three longer pieces together using backstitch or mattress stitch, then attach the shorter piece but only sew halfway up the seam in order to create an opening for the fruit. Attach one button on each side of the opening on the main piece. On the shorter piece, attach yarn and make a loop at each edge just large enough to close around the buttons.

Egg cozies

Keep your boiled eggs nice and warm with these eye-catching egg cozy covers—what could be more fun, frivolous, and funky? The pretty kid mohair frill and bobble on top add the finishing touches to this ever-so-saucy design. You should be able to knit two or three egg cozies from the recommended quantities of yarn.

THE KNITTY GRITTY

Size: To fit standard-size egg.
Yarn: Fingering-weight blend (70% super kid mohair, 30% silk; 229 yd [210 m] per 25 g ball): red (yarn A) for frill and bobble, 1 ball. Fingering-weight wool (100% merino wool; 191 yd [175 m] per 50 g ball): pink-red (yarn B) for egg cozy, 1 ball.
Needles: Size 3 (3.25 mm).
Notions: Tapestry needle.
Gauge: 28 sts x 36 rows = 4" (10 cm) in stockinette stitch using size 3 (3.25 mm) needles. Exact gauge isn't necessary.

Abbreviations
k—knit
k1f&b—knit into front and back of stitch
p—purl
psso—pass slip stitch over
RS—right side
sl 1—slip 1 stitch
tog—together
WS—wrong side

Frill

Using size 3 (3.25 mm) needles and yarn A, cast on 228 sts.
Row 1: (RS) Knit.
Row 2: *Sl 1, p2tog, psso, repeat from * to end (76 sts).
Row 3: *K2tog, repeat from * to end (38 sts).
Cut yarn A.

Cover

Rows 4–12: Join yarn B and, starting with a purl row, work nine rows in stockinette stitch.
Row 13: K9, k2tog, k16, k2tog, k9 (36 sts).
Row 14: Purl.
Row 15: K9, k2tog, k14, k2tog, k9 (34 sts).
Row 16: Purl.
Row 17: K9, k2tog, k12, k2tog, k9 (32 sts).
Row 18: Purl.
Row 19: K9, k2tog, k10, k2tog, k9 (30 sts).
Row 20: Purl.
Row 21: *K3, k2tog, repeat from * to end (24 sts).
Row 22: Purl.
Row 23: *K2, k2tog, repeat from * to end (18 sts).
Row 24: Purl.
Row 25: *K2tog, repeat from * to end (9 sts).
Row 26: Purl.
Break off yarn B, leaving a 4" (10 cm) tail. Thread a tapestry needle with the tail and insert through the remaining sts. Pull gently on yarn tail to close top of cozy and fasten off.

Bobble

Using size 3 (3.25 mm) needles and yarn A, cast on 1 st.
Row 1: K1f&b twice, k1 into same st (5 sts).
Rows 2, 4, and 6: Purl.
Rows 3 and 5: Knit.
Row 7: K2tog, k1, k2tog (3 sts).
Row 8: P3tog.
Cut yarn A, leaving a 4" (10 cm) tail. Thread the tail through the remaining st, and fasten off.

Tip

When casting on such a large number of stitches, place a stitch marker after every 25 stitches to make counting easier. This is very useful when using such fine yarn.

Finishing

With a tapestry needle, weave in the loose yarn tails to WS of work. Fold the cozy in half and sew the wool section of the back seam using backstitch or mattress stitch. Use a flat seam for the mohair frill section to stop the seam from showing. Stitch the bobble to the top of the cozy with the cast-on and bind-off edges of the bobble together.

Washcloths

Soft and simple, these washcloths are a great way to practice your increasing and decreasing techniques. The first version is worked in a bulky-weight chenille yarn and knitted in garter stitch throughout, so it's really quick and easy to make and the uneven texture of the chenille adds a rustic charm to the design. The second version uses a cotton tape yarn for a bulkier, tighter weave cloth. The soft chenille makes an ideal face cloth, while the cotton tape is more suitable as an exfoliating body cloth.

THE KNITTY GRITTY

Size: About 8" (20.5 cm) wide x 9½" (24 cm) long.
Yarn: Chenille washcloth: Bulky-weight cotton chenille (100% cotton chenille; 153 yd [140 m] per 100 g ball): 1 ball. Cotton washcloth: Bulky-weight cotton tape (100% cotton; 33 yd [30 m] per 50 g ball): 1 ball.
Needles: Size 6 (4 mm) for chenille cloth; size 15 (10 mm) for cotton cloth.
Notions: Tapestry needle.
Gauge: 17 sts x 38 rows = 4" (10 cm) in garter stitch using size 6 (4 mm) needles for chenille cloth; 10 sts x 18 rows = 4" (10 cm) in garter stitch using size 15 (10 mm) needles for cotton cloth. Exact gauge isn't necessary.

Abbreviations
k—knit
m1—make 1 stitch by picking up horizontal strand before next stitch with right needle, slipping it onto left needle, and knitting through back of loop
psso—pass slip stitch over
sl 1—slip 1 stitch
tog—together

Chenille cloth

The pattern is worked in garter stitch throughout. Using size 6 (4 mm) needles and chenille yarn, cast on 3 sts.
Row 1: Knit.
Row 2: K1, m1, k1, m1, k1 (5 sts).
Rows 3–4: Knit.
Row 5: K1, m1, knit until 1 st remains, m1, k1.
Repeat rows 3–5 until there are 33 sts or until the required width is achieved. Knit two rows without increasing.
Next row: K1, sl 1, k1, psso, knit to last 3 sts, k2tog, k1.
Knit two rows without decreasing.
Repeat last three rows until 3 sts remain,

ending after the final two knit rows without decreases are worked. Bind off knitwise.

Finishing

With a tapestry needle, weave in the loose yarn tails to one side of work.

Cotton cloth

Using size 15 (10 mm) needles and cotton tape yarn, work as instructed for the chenille washcloth, but only increase until there are 17 sts instead of 33. Knit the next two rows without increasing, then start decreasing until 3 sts remain. Bind off knitwise. Finish as for the chenille washcloth.

Plastic wash bag

You don't have to use regular yarn for knitting. There are all sorts of materials you can use—wire, ribbons, shoelaces, videotape, even panty hose. All you have to do is tie strips of these materials together and you can start knitting. Why not recycle your old plastic bags to create this brightly colored wash bag? Collect as many different colors of bags as you can and watch the random pattern emerge.

Making plastic yarn

Make plastic yarn by cutting bags into strips and knotting them together to form one long continuous length. Lay the plastic bag flat, getting rid of any big creases. With a pair of sharp scissors, cut down the middle from top to bottom. Cut each piece down the middle once more. Depending on the design of the plastic bag, either cut through the handles at the top to make a flat strip or cut off that section of plastic and discard. Open out the strips to full length and knot together. The knots will form a decorative feature in the knitted fabric.

Panels

Using size 15 (10 mm) needles, cast on 20 sts.
Row 1: (RS) Knit.
Row 2: Purl.
Rows 1–2 form a stockinette fabric. Repeat both rows until the work measures about 12" (30.5 cm) from the cast-on edge.
Bind off knitwise.
Make a second panel in the same way.

Handle

Using size 15 (10 mm) needles, cast on 6 sts.
Row 1: (RS) Knit.
Row 2: Purl.
Repeat these two rows until the handle measures about 14" (35.5 cm) long.
Bind off knitwise.

Finishing

Thread a sewing needle with about a 20" (51 cm) length of strong sewing thread. Place both bag panels right sides together and sew along three of the edges using backstitch; rethread the needle as necessary. Turn the bag right side out and stitch the handle in place to the open edge of the bag as follows: *With right sides of handle facing, center one end of the handle on the outside of one panel, about 1½" (4 cm) from the top edge. With sewing needle and thread, sew the handle in place using backstitch. Repeat from * on the second panel with opposite end of handle (see photo).

THE KNITTY GRITTY

Size: 10" (25.5 cm) wide x 12" (30.5 cm) high.
Materials: About 30 plastic bags, each cut into four strips and then knotted together to form a long length of plastic "yarn." Add more bags if necessary.
Needles: Size 15 (10 mm).
Notions: Strong sewing thread and sewing needle.
Gauge: 8 sts x 10 rows = 4" (10 cm) in stockinette stitch using size 15 (10 mm) needles. Exact gauge isn't necessary.

Abbreviations
k—knit
p—purl
RS—right side

Cozy toe slippers

These simple slippers are thick, warm, and great for relaxing. You certainly won't get cold toes if you wear these on an icy winter's day. The super bulky merino yarn felts beautifully in the washing machine to create a soft, simple, but durable fabric. The button strap provides a subtle decorative detail.

THE KNITTY GRITTY

Size: Slipper sole length (after felting): 9½" (24 cm). The finished size will vary depending on the amount of felting.

Yarn: Super-bulky wool (100% merino wool; 87 yd [80 m] per 100 g ball): 2 balls.

Needles: Size 17 (12 mm). Adjust needle size if necessary to obtain correct gauge.

Notions: Tapestry needle; two 1" (25 mm) long toggle buttons; matching color sewing thread and sewing needle to attach buttons.

Gauge: 8 sts x 10 rows = 4" (10 cm) in stockinette stitch using size 17 (12 mm) needles before felting.

Abbreviations
k—knit
p—purl
psso—pass slip stitch over
RS—right side
sl 1—slip 1 stitch
st(s)—stitch(es)
tbl—through back of loop
tog—together
WS—wrong side
yo—yarnover

Sole

Using size 17 (12 mm) needles, cast on 40 sts.

Row 1: (RS) K1, yo, k18, yo, k1, yo, k1, yo, k18, yo, k1 (45 sts).

Row 2: K1, k1 tbl, k18, k1 tbl, k1, k1 tbl, k1, k1 tbl, k18, k1 tbl, k1.

Row 3: K2, yo, k18, yo, k2, yo, k3, yo, k18, yo, k2 (50 sts).

Row 4: K2, k1 tbl, k18, k1 tbl, k3, k1 tbl, k2, , k1 tbl, k18, k1 tbl, k2.

Row 5: K3, yo, k18, yo, k4, yo, k4, yo, k18, yo, k3 (55 sts).

Row 6: K3, k1 tbl, k18, k1 tbl, k4, k1 tbl, k4, k1 tbl, k18, k1 tbl, k3.

Upper

Rows 7–10: Starting with a knit row, work four rows in stockinette stitch.

Begin short rows:

Row 11: (RS) K31, k2tog tbl, turn.

Row 12: Sl 1 purlwise, p7, p2tog, turn.

Row 13: Sl 1 purlwise, k7, k2tog tbl, turn.

Repeat rows 12–13 until 16 sts remain on the left needle after a WS row. Do not turn the work.

Next row: Purl the 16 remaining sts from left needle. End of short rows.

Next three rows: Knit. Bind off knitwise. Cut the yarn, leaving a 4" (10 cm) tail.

Strap

From the last decrease on the upper, count back 8 sts, then with RS facing, join yarn and pick up and knit 3 sts just under the bind-off edge of the slipper. Knit eighteen rows.

Buttonhole row: K1, yo, k2tog. Knit two rows.

Next row: Sl 1, k2tog, psso. Cut the yarn, leaving a 4" (10 cm) tail, pass it through the last st, and pull tight to fasten off.

Make a second slipper and strap the same way. Join this strap on the opposite side of the second slipper, so the straps on each slipper button are on the outside of the feet (see photos).

Finishing

With a tapestry needle, weave in the loose yarn tails to WS of work. Place the ends of the heel and sole together along the cast-on edge and sew together using mattress stitch. Felt the slippers (see right). If possible, try them on the intended wearer's feet before the slippers are completely dry. With sewing thread and needle, sew the buttons into place for fastening the straps.

Felting

This is a process of shrinking a woolen fabric by washing it in soapy water to bind the fibers together to create a more solid and fluffy fabric. It can be done by hand but is easier in a washing machine. Felting is very much a case of trial and error, because the water temperature and agitation strength of each washing machine varies. Always experiment with a knitted swatch before placing the finished item into the machine. Felting will not work with superwash wools, cottons, or synthetic yarns. Place the finished item in a washing machine with a hard-wearing fabric such as an old pair of jeans or a denim jacket (if using a dark color yarn) or a few old tennis balls. Set the washing machine on the hottest cycle and fill the tub with hot water. Add a small amount of your usual washing detergent; using just enough to make the water feel slippery. Too many suds may impede felting. The felting process may require more than one cycle to reach the desired stage. When the cycle is complete, ease the damp item into the required shape by patting, pulling, and smoothing as necessary. Allow to air dry.

Snuggle blanket

This blanket is modern and funky and can be used anywhere. Wrap yourself up in the beautifully textured soft fabric and you won't ever want to leave it behind. The cable moves in and out, flowing across the fabric. The snuggle blanket is knitted in a bulky merino wool and alpaca blend yarn in a contemporary marled shade.

THE KNITTY GRITTY

Size: 42 x 50" (106.5 x 127 cm).

Yarn: Bulky-weight blend (42% merino wool, 30% acrylic, 28% superfine alpaca; 109 yd [100 m] per 100 g ball): 9 balls.

Needles: Size 10½ (6.5 mm); size 11 (8 mm); cable needle. Adjust needle size if necessary to obtain correct gauge.

Notions: Tapestry needle.

Gauge: 11 sts x 17 rows = 4" (10 cm) in stockinette stitch using size 11 (8 mm) needles.

Abbreviations

k—knit
p—purl
RS—right side
tbl—through back of loop
WS—wrong side

Chart

Row numbers (right side): 45, 43, 41, 39, 37, 35, 33, 31, 29, 27, 25, 23, 21, 19, 17, 15, 13, 11, 9, 7

Note

The first and last 4 stitches in each row and not included in chart. See page 84 for instructions on how to work these stitches as well as how to work the chart.

Key

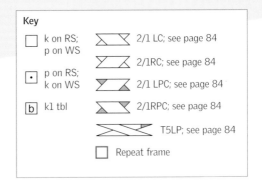

- ☐ k on RS; p on WS
- ⚫ p on RS; k on WS
- b k1 tbl
- 2/1 LC; see page 84
- 2/1RC; see page 84
- 2/1 LPC; see page 84
- 2/1RPC; see page 84
- T5LP; see page 84
- ☐ Repeat frame

Cabling techniques

Left-cross cable (2/1LC)
Slip the next two stitches onto a cable needle, hold the cable needle at the front of the work, knit the next stitch from left needle, then knit the two stitches from the cable needle.

Right-cross cable (2/1RC)
Slip the next stitch onto a cable needle, hold the cable needle at the back of the work, knit the next two stitches from left needle, then knit the stitch from the cable needle.

Left-cross purl cable (2/1LPC)
Slip the next two stitches onto a cable needle, hold the cable needle at the front of the work, purl the next stitch from the left needle, then knit the two stitches from the cable needle.

Right-cross purl cable (2/1RPC)
Slip the next stitch onto a cable needle, hold the cable needle at the back of the work, knit the next two stitches from left needle, then purl the stitch from the cable needle.

Twist 5 left purl (T5LP)
Slip the next two stitches onto a cable needle, hold the cable needle at the front of the work, (p1, k2) from the left needle, then knit the two stitches from the cable needle.

First border

Using size 10½ (6.5 mm) needles, cast on 113 sts.
Rows 1–4: Knit. This forms the garter stitch border. Change to size 11 (8 mm) needles.
Row 5: K2, p2 (these first 4 sts form side border), p6, k4, p5, *p1, k3, p7, k3, p7, k4, p5**, repeat from * to ** two more times, p2, k2 (these last 4 sts form side border).
Row 6: K4 (these first 4 sts form side border), *k5, p4, k7, p3, k7, p3, k1**, repeat from * to ** two more times, k5, p4, k6, k4 (these last 4 sts form side border).

Cable design

Note: The first and last 4 sts in each row are not shown on chart. Work these sts as established for border. Begin chart with row 7 and work the 40 chart rows four times as follows: On RS rows, k2, p2, work the next 15 chart sts once, then work the following 30 sts within the red repeat frame three times, end row with p2, k2. On WS rows, k4, work the next 30 sts three times, then work next 15 sts once, k4 to end row.
Rows 167–168: Repeat rows 5–6. Change to size 10½ (6.5 mm) needles.
Rows 169–172: Knit. Bind off purlwise.

Finishing

With a tapestry needle, weave in the loose yarn tails to WS of work. Block and press to the required size.

Felted buttons

Can't find buttons to match your garment? Why not make your own? These buttons are funky to wear and take minutes to knit. They are worked in DK-weight pure new wool and then felted to add structure and shape. Single-color and two-color buttons are pictured here, but you could knit multicolored ones to make a bolder fashion statement.

THE KNITTY GRITTY

Size: About 2" (5 cm) diameter.
Yarn: Scraps of DK-weight wool (100% pure new wool) in various colors. Note: Don't use superwash wools or synthetic yarns because these yarns will not felt.
Needles: Size 8 (5 mm).
Notions: Tapestry needle.
Gauge: Not important.

Abbreviations
k1f&b—knit into front and back of stitch
st(s)—stitch(es)
WS—wrong side

Single-color button
Using size 8 (5 mm) needles, cast on 8 sts.
Row 1: (WS) Purl.
Row 2: K1f&b in every st (16 sts).
Row 3: Purl.
Row 4: Repeat row 2 (32 sts).
Row 5: Purl.
Row 6: Knit.
Bind off knitwise.

Two-color button

Work as for the single-color button, but bind off using a contrasting shade of yarn. You could also work in stripes throughout, using different colors for each row.

Finishing

With a tapestry needle, weave in the loose yarn tails to WS of work and sew the short edges together to form a circle. Felt the buttons (see page 81), then sew them onto the garment of your choice.

Houndstooth dog coat

Keep your canine pal protected from the elements in the utmost style. The dog coat fabric is knitted in pure new wool and features a houndstooth check pattern worked using the Fair Isle technique in two bright colors for impact. The simple ribbed collar can be easily popped over the head of your pooch, and the body of the coat has a buttonhole fastening.

THE KNITTY GRITTY

Size: To fit small dog. Circumference around buttoned section: about 22" (56 cm). Collar circumference: about 13" (33 cm). Upper panel: about 8½" (21.5 cm) long x 10¼" (26 cm) wide excluding button panels. Lower panel: about 6" (15 cm) long x 8½" (21.5 cm) wide.
Yarn: DK-weight wool (100% pure new wool; 123 yd [112.5 m] per 50 g ball); red (yarn A), 2 balls; blue (yarn B), 1 ball.
Needles: Size 5 (3.75 mm); size 7 (4.5 mm). Adjust needle size if necessary to obtain correct gauge.
Notions: Tapestry needle; six ⅝" (15 mm) buttons; sewing thread and needle if the holes in the buttons are too small to use yarn.
Gauge: 22 sts x 26 rows = 4" (10 cm) in Fair Isle pattern using size 7 (4.5 mm) needles.

Abbreviations
k—knit
p—purl
RS—right side
st(s)—stitch(es)
WS—wrong side

Lower panel

Using size 5 (3.75 mm) needles and yarn A, cast on 40 sts.
Row 1: (RS) *K2, p2, repeat from * to end.
Work row 1 for a total of 4 rows.
Change to size 7 (4.5 mm) needles and join yarn B. Working in stockinette stitch, begin the lower panel chart repeating rows 1–4 of houndstooth pattern until work measures about 6" (15 cm) in length from cast-on edge, ending with a WS row. Using yarn A, bind off knitwise.

Upper panel

Using size 5 (3.75 mm) needles and yarn A, cast on 52 sts.
Rows 1–4: Work in k2, p2 rib same as for lower panel. Change to size 7 (4.5 mm) needles and join yarn B. Working in stockinette stitch, begin the upper panel chart repeating houndstooth pattern rows 1–4 until work measures about 8½" (21.5 cm) in length from cast-on edge, ending with a WS row. Using yarn A, bind off knitwise.

Lower panel side edging

With RS facing and using size 5 (3.75 mm) needles and yarn A, pick up and knit 38 sts along one side edge of the panel.
Row 1 (WS): K2, *p2, k2, repeat from * to end.
Row 2: P2, *k2, p2, repeat from * to end.
Rows 3–5: Repeat rows 1–2, then row 1 again.
Bind off in rib pattern. Repeat along the second side edge of the lower panel.

Upper panel side edging

With RS facing and using size 5 (3.75 mm) needles and yarn A, pick up and knit 54 sts along one side edge of upper panel, starting at the cast-on edge.
Rows 1–5: Work in ribbing as instructed for rows 1–5 of lower panel side edging.
Row 6 (RS): Bind off 16 sts in rib pattern, counting the stitch already on the right needle, rib 18 sts, bind off remaining sts. Break off yarn and rejoin to 18 sts.

Lower panel chart

Upper panel chart

Key

Yarn A

Yarn B

Repeat frame

Fold-over seams

For fold-over collars and cuffs, the seams need to be reversed halfway along for a neat finish.

1 With wrong sides together, starting at the bound-off edge of the collar, slip-stitch the first half of the seam. Work along the stitch edges so that the double rib pattern is maintained along the seam. Pull to tighten the last stitch.

2 Turn the work right sides together and bring the needle through to the wrong side of the work. Continue to slip-stitch along the seam, now working from the wrong side.

Rows 7–17: Work 11 rows in ribbing.

Row 18 (buttonhole row 1): Rib 2, bind off next 2 sts, counting the st already on the right needle, rib 4, bind off next 2 sts, counting the st already on the right needle, rib 4, bind off next 2 sts, counting the st already on the right needle, rib 2.

Row 19 (buttonhole row 2): Rib 2, cast on 2 sts, rib 4, cast on 2 sts, rib 4, cast on 2 sts, rib 2.

Rows 20–21: Work two more rows in ribbing. Bind off in rib pattern. With RS facing and using size 5 (3.75 mm) needles and yarn A, pick up and knit 54 sts along the second side edge of upper panel, starting at the bind-off edge. Work as for first side edge except:

Row 6: Bind off 20 sts in rib pattern, counting the stitch already on the right needle, rib 18, bind off remaining sts in rib pattern.

Collar

With RS facing and using size 5 (3.75 mm) needles and yarn A, pick up and knit 46 sts from the bind-off edge of the upper panel and 38 sts from the bind-off edge of the lower panel (84 sts). Work back and forth in rib pattern as follows:

Next row: K2, p2; repeat from * to end of row.

Repeat row 1 until ribbing measures 4¾" (12 cm).

Bind off in rib pattern.

Finishing

With a tapestry needle, weave in the loose yarn tails to WS of work. Block and press all the pieces. Sew the fold-over collar seam, slip-stitching 3" (7.5 cm) with WS together, then completing the seam with RS together (see step-by-step sequence on page 88). Attach buttons to the lower panel to match the buttonholes.

Coats for big dogs

This coat is designed to fit a small dog, but it can easily be adapted for a large one. The two main pieces are simply rectangles and can be lengthened or widened very easily, or the buttonhole straps may be lengthened. The Fair Isle pattern is a four-row and four-stitch repeat, so any variations should be in multiples of four. If you widen the pattern, pick up more stitches around the neck when working the collar.

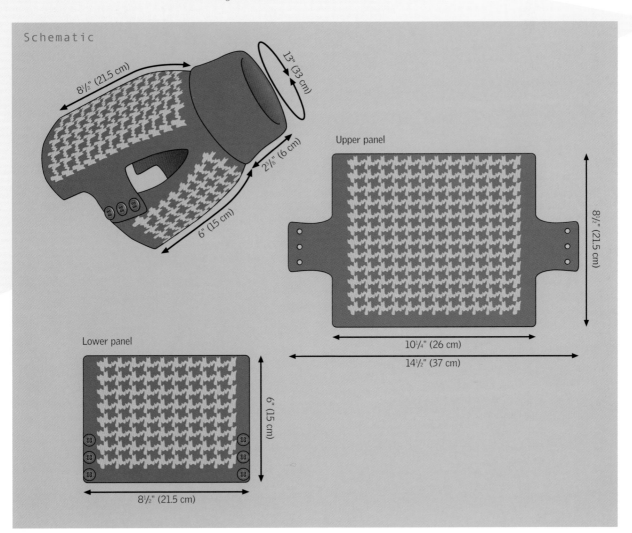

Schematic

8½" (21.5 cm)

13" (33 cm)

2⅜" (6 cm)

6" (15 cm)

Upper panel

8½" (21.5 cm)

10¼" (26 cm)

14½" (37 cm)

Lower panel

6" (15 cm)

8½" (21.5 cm)

Easy-care cacti

No green fingers are needed for these cacti—
they're what you could call really low-maintenance
gardening. The shapes of real cacti are easily and
convincingly reproduced, worked in
simple ribbing and seed stitch, then
stuffed and placed in the smallest
of plant pots with tiny pebbles
to add to the effect.

THE KNITTY GRITTY

Size: 3–4" (7.5–10 cm) high.
Yarn: Beaded cactus:
Aran-weight blend (70%
lambswool, 26% kid mohair,
4% nylon; 153 yd [140 m]
per 50 g ball): green, 1 ball.
Seed stitch cactus: DK-
weight blend (50% wool,
50% cotton; 123 yd [113 m]
per 50 g ball): green, 1 ball.
Needles: Size 6 (4 mm);
size 3 (3.25 mm).
Notions: Tapestry needle;
fifty 3 mm beads; matching
color sewing thread and
sewing needle to use when
attaching beads; polyester
fiberfill; two small plant
pots; sufficient cardboard
to cut a disk that will fit
into the top of each plant
pot; two popsicle sticks; glue
(optional); small pebbles.
Gauge: Not important.

Abbreviations
k—knit
p—purl
RS—right side
tog—together
WS—wrong side

Beaded cactus

Using size 6 (4 mm) needles
and Aran-weight yarn, cast
on 34 sts.
Row 1: (RS) K2, *p2, k2,
repeat from * to end.
Row 2: P2, *k2, p2, repeat
from * to end.
Repeat rows 1–2 until cactus
measures 3" (7.5 cm), finishing
on a WS row.
Next row: K2tog, *p2tog,
k2tog, repeat from * to end
(17 sts).
Cut the yarn, leaving a 12"
(30.5 cm) tail.

Finishing

Thread a tapestry needle
with the yarn tail and thread
through the stitches on the
needle. Remove the stitches
from the needle and gently pull
the length of yarn to gather
the stitches together and close
the cactus top. With right
sides together, use this same
length of yarn and backstitch
or mattress stitch to sew the
sides of the cactus together to
form a closed tube. Thread a
sewing needle with sewing
thread and randomly sew
beads down the center of the
knit stitches (see page 65).
Stuff the cactus with fiberfill
and mold it into shape.

Seed stitch cactus

To make the large central piece, use size 3 (3.25 mm) needles and DK-weight yarn to cast on 13 sts.

Row 1: (RS) K1, *p1, k1 repeat from * to end.

Repeat row 1 another 39 times.

Bind off knitwise.

To make the two branches, use size 3 (3.25 mm) needles and DK-weight yarn to cast on 9 sts for each. Work as instructed for the large piece, completing 42 rows for one branch and 24 rows for the other.

Finishing

Fold the seed stitch rectangles in half and sew the sides and top using backstitch or mattress stitch. Stuff the larger piece with fiberfill, but do not use too much because the cactus should remain fairly flat. Sew the smaller pieces onto the larger piece (the branches are not stuffed).

Potting the cacti

Prepare a plant pot for each cactus as illustrated below. Slip the cactus onto the popsicle stick; glue the cactus in place on the cardboard base if you wish. Carefully insert the cardboard disk into the plant pot so that it sits just below the lip of the pot. Sprinkle small pebbles onto the cardboard to cover it.

Preparing the plant pot

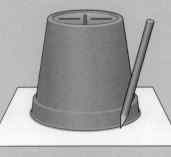

1 Cut a circular piece of cardboard to fit into the lip of a small plant pot.

2 Cut a small "X" in the center of the cardboard circle.

3 Insert a popsicle stick through the "X", leaving 1–2" (2.5–5 cm) above the cardboard to support the cactus.

chapter 5

PUNK GARAGE ROCKS

There is a wannabe rock star in all of us — this chapter will bring it out in the open. For all you listeners out there, carry your vinyl around in the record bag, then flop down and rest your head on the musical pillow as you listen to your favorite tracks. If you are a real player, look the part in the deconstructed safety-pin sweater while carrying your guitar in its soft cotton case from gig to gig.

Safety-pin sweater

This two-tone stripy sweater is big, baggy, and bumble-bee bold. The randomly placed horizontal slashes between the stripes are held together with safety pins to make you stand out from the crowd wherever you go. You can position the slashes as indicated in the pattern or place them wherever you like to make the sweater truly individual.

THE KNITTY GRITTY

Size: Chest: 46" (117 cm)
Length: 26½" (67.5 cm).
Yarn: Super-bulky weight wool (100% merino wool; 87 yd [80 m] per 100 g ball): brown (yarn A), 5 balls; yellow (yarn B), 4 balls.
Needles: Size 17 (12 mm). Adjust needle size if necessary to obtain correct gauge.
Notions: Stitch holder; tapestry needle; about two dozen safety pins.
Gauge: 8 sts x 12 rows = 4" (10 cm) in stockinette stitch using size 17 (12 mm) needles.

Abbreviations
k—knit
k1f&b—knit into front and back of stitch
p—purl
RS—right side
WS—wrong side

Back

The sweater is worked in a striped sequence throughout, as follows: 8 rows yarn A; 6 rows yarn B.
Using size 17 (12 mm) needles and yarn A, cast on 46 sts.
Rows 1–13: Maintaining the stripe sequence and starting with a knit row, work in stockinette stitch.
Row 14: (WS) P22, bind off 10 sts purlwise, purl to end.
Row 15: K14, cast on 10 sts, knit to end.
Rows 16–21: Work in stockinette stitch, starting with a purl row.
Row 22: P10, bind off 15 sts purlwise, purl to end.
Row 23: K21, cast on 15 sts, knit to end.
Rows 24–35: Work in stockinette stitch, starting with a purl row.
Row 36: P30, bind off 10 sts purlwise, purl to end.
Row 37: K6, cast on 10 sts, knit to end.
Rows 38–44: Work in stockinette stitch, starting with a purl row.

Armholes

Continue in stockinette stitch, starting with a knit row.
Rows 45–46: Bind off 3 sts at beginning of next two rows (40 sts).
Row 47: K1, k2tog, knit to last 3 sts, skpo, k1 (38 sts).
Row 48: P1, p2tog tbl, purl to last 3 sts, p2tog, p1 (36 sts).
Row 49: Repeat row 47 (34 sts).
Rows 50–55: Work in stockinette stitch, starting with a purl row.
Row 56: P4 sts, bind off 9 sts purlwise, purl to end.
Row 57: K21, cast on 9 sts, knit to end.
Starting with a purl row, continue straight in stockinette stitch until armhole measures 10" (26 cm), ending with a WS row. Keep a note of how many rows you work to reach this length.

Shoulders and back neck

Bind off 3 sts at beginning of the next two rows (28 sts).
Row 3: Bind off 3 sts knitwise, knit until there are 6 sts on right needle, bind off 10 sts knitwise for back neck, knit to end of row (9 sts on one shoulder, 6 sts on the other).
Row 4: Bind off 3 sts purlwise, purl to neck edge.
Row 5: Bind off 3 sts knitwise at neck edge, knit to end.
Row 6: Bind off remaining 3 sts purlwise.
With WS facing, rejoin yarn to remaining sts at neck edge.
Row 1: Bind off 3 sts purlwise, purl to end.
Row 2: Bind off remaining 3 sts knitwise.

Front

Work as instructed for back until you have worked six rows less than the back up to the shoulder shaping, ending with a WS row (34 sts remain).

Shoulders and front neck

Row 1: K14, bind off 6 sts knitwise, knit to end.
Row 2: P12, p2tog.
Row 3: K2tog, k11.
Row 4: P10, p2tog.
Row 5: K2tog, k9.
Row 6: P8, p2tog.
Row 7: Knit.
Row 8: Bind off 3 sts purlwise, purl to end.
Rows 9–10: Repeat rows 7–8.
Row 11: Knit.
Bind off remaining 3 sts purlwise.
With WS facing, rejoin yarn to remaining sts at neck edge.
Row 2: P2tog, p12.
Row 3: K11, k2tog.
Row 4: P2tog, p10.

Row 5: K9, k2tog.
Row 6: P2tog, p8.
Row 7: Bind off 3 sts knitwise, knit to end.
Row 8: Purl.
Rows 9–10: Repeat rows 7–8.
Bind off remaining 3 sts knitwise.

Sleeve 1

Using size 17 (12 mm) needles and yarn A, cast on 24 sts. Work in stockinette stitch throughout, maintaining the stripe sequence as before. The following instructions are for the shaping and pattern rows only.
Row 8: P6, bind off 6 sts purlwise, purl to end.
Row 9: K12, cast on 6 sts, knit to end.
Row 13: K1f&b, knit to last st, k1f&b (26 sts).
Row 19: Repeat row 13 (28 sts).
Row 22: P16, bind off 6 sts purlwise, purl to end.
Row 23: K6, cast on 6 sts, knit to end.
Row 25: Repeat row 13 (30 sts).
Row 31: Repeat row 13 (32 sts).
Row 36: P9, bind off 6 sts purlwise, purl to end.
Row 37: K1f&b, k16, cast on 6 sts, knit to last st, k1f&b (34 sts).
Rows 41, 45, 49: Repeat row 13 (40 sts).

Schematic

3½" (9 cm)

26½" (67.5 cm)

18½" (47 cm)

23" (58.5 cm)

Sleeve cap shaping

Continue straight until the sleeve measures 18½" (47 cm), ending with a WS row.
Row 3: K2tog, knit to last 2 sts, k2tog (38 sts).
Row 4: Purl.
Rows 5–8: Repeat rows 3–4 twice (34 sts).
Bind off knitwise.

Sleeve 2

Cast on as for sleeve 1. Work in stockinette stitch and maintain the stripe sequence as for sleeve 1, but place the slashes and shapings as follows:
Row 13: K1f&b, knit to last st, k1f&b (26 sts).
Row 14: P8, bind off 6 sts purlwise, purl to end.
Row 15: K12, cast on 6 sts, knit to end.
Row 19: Repeat row 13 (28 sts).
Row 25: Repeat row 13 (30 sts).
Row 28: P14, bind off 6 sts purlwise, purl to end.
Row 29: K10, cast on 6 sts, knit to end.
Row 31, 37, 41: Repeat row 13 (36 sts).
Row 42: P8, bind off 6 sts purlwise, purl to end.
Row 43: K22, cast on 6 sts, knit to end.
Rows 45 and 49: Repeat row 13 (40 sts).
Continue cap shaping as for sleeve 1.

Preparing the pieces

With a tapestry needle, weave in the loose yarn tails to WS of work. Block and press all the pieces. Join the right shoulder seam using backstitch.

Neck trim

Using size 17 (12 mm) needles and yarn A, and with RS facing, pick up and knit 11 sts down left side of neck, 6 sts across front neck, 11 sts up right side of neck, and 18 sts across back neck (46 sts).
Row 1: P2, *k2, p2, repeat from * to end.
Row 2: K2, *p2, k2, repeat from * to end.
Rows 3–4: Repeat rows 1–2.
Rows 5–9: Starting with a knit row, work in stockinette stitch.
Bind off very loosely purlwise.

Finishing

With a tapestry needle and using backstitch, join the left shoulder seam. Sew the sleeve caps into the armholes; leaving a 3" (7.5 cm) slash at the front of one armhole. Join the side and sleeve seams using backstitch. Join the neck trim seam using slip stitch. Attach safety pins to the slashes wherever you like.

Guitar case

This guitar case is worked in a machine-washable Aran-weight cotton and microfiber blend yarn. It is soft, portable, and perfect for protecting your guitar from the knocks and bumps of the rock'n'roll lifestyle. It has sturdy handles for carrying your guitar around and a zipper fastening at the bottom for easy access.

THE KNITTY GRITTY

Size: To fit average acoustic guitar. Total length: 38" (96.5 cm). Widest part: 18¼" (46.5 cm).
Yarn: Aran-weight blend (55% cotton, 45% microfiber; 97 yd [89 m] per 50 g ball): gray, 12 balls.
Needles: Size 6 (4 mm); size 8 (5 mm). Adjust needle size if necessary to obtain correct gauge.
Notions: Open-style stitch markers; tapestry needle; approx. 1½ yds (1.5 m) gray medium-weight lining fabric; sewing needle and thread; 18" (45.5 cm) long closed-end zipper.
Gauge: 16 sts x 23 rows = 4" (10 cm) in stockinette stitch using size 8 (5 mm) needles.

Abbreviations
k—knit
k1f&b—knit into front and back of stitch
p—purl
p1f&b—purl into front and back of stitch
RS—right side
skpo—slip 1 stitch, knit 1 stitch, pass slip stitch over
tog—together
WS—wrong side

Front panel
Using size 8 (5 mm) needles, cast on 46 sts.
Row 1: (RS) Knit.
Row 2: P1f&b, purl to last 2 sts, p1f&b, p1 (48 sts).
Row 3: K1f&b, knit to last 2 sts, k1f&b, k1 (50 sts).
Rows 4–9: Repeat rows 2–3 three times (62 sts).
Row 10: Purl.
Row 11: K1f&b, knit to last 2 sts, k1f&b, k1 (64 sts).
Rows 12–17: Repeat rows 10–11 three times (70 sts).
Rows 18–22: Work in stockinette stitch, starting with a purl row.
Row 23: Repeat row 3 (72 sts).
Rows 24–26: Work in stockinette stitch, starting with a purl row.
Row 27: Repeat row 3 (74 sts).
Rows 28–44: Work in stockinette stitch, starting with a purl row.
Row 45: K1, skpo, knit to last 3 sts, k2tog, k1 (72 sts).

Rows 46–50: Work in stockinette stitch, starting with a purl row.
Rows 51–56: Repeat rows 45–50 (70 sts).
Row 57: Repeat row 45 (68 sts).
Rows 58–64: Work in stockinette stitch, starting with a purl row.
Row 65: Repeat row 45 (66 sts).
Rows 66–97: Repeat rows 58–65 four times (58 sts).
Rows 98–102: Work in stockinette stitch, starting with a purl row.
Row 103: Repeat row 45, placing a marker at beginning of row for handle (56 sts).
Rows 104–115: Repeat rows 98–103 twice, placing a marker at end of row 110 for handle (50 sts).
Rows 116–118: Work in stockinette stitch, starting with a purl row.
Row 119: Repeat row 45 (50 sts).
Rows 120–123: Repeat rows 116–119 (48 sts).

Row 124: Purl.

Row 125: K1, skpo, knit to last 3 sts, k2tog, k1, placing marker at beginning of row for handle (46 sts).

Row 126: P1, p2tog, purl to last 3 sts, p2tog tbl, p1 (44 sts).

Rows 127–130: Repeat rows 125–126 twice (36 sts).

Row 131: Knit.

Row 132: Repeat row 126, placing a marker at end of row for handle (34 sts).

Rows 133–208: Work even in stockinette stitch, starting with a knit row, and placing a marker at each end of row 133 for side panel insertion.

Top shaping

Row 209: K1, skpo, knit to last 3 sts, k2tog, k1 (32 sts).

Rows 210–212: Work in stockinette stitch, starting with a purl row.

Row 213: Repeat row 209 (30 sts).

Row 214: Purl.

Row 215: Repeat row 209 (28 sts).

Rows 216–218: Work in stockinette stitch, starting with a purl row.

Row 219: Repeat row 209 (26 sts).

Row 220: P1, p2tog, purl to last 3 sts, p2tog tbl, p1 (24 sts).

Rows 221–222: Repeat rows 219–220 (20 sts).

Row 223: Repeat row 219 (18 sts). Bind off purlwise.

Make another panel for the back of the guitar case in the same way, placing handle markers at opposite ends of rows 103, 110, 125, and 132 and side panel markers at each end of row 133.

Side panels

Using size 8 (5 mm) needles, cast on 22 sts.

Rows 1–20: Work in stockinette stitch, starting with a knit row.

Row 21: (RS) K2tog, k18, k2tog (20 sts).

Rows 22–44: Work in stockinette stitch, starting with a purl row.

Row 45: K2tog, k16, k2tog (18 sts).

Rows 46–56: Work in stockinette stitch, starting with a purl row.

Row 57: K2tog, k14, k2tog (16 sts).

Rows 58–64: Work in stockinette stitch, starting with a purl row.

Row 65: K2tog, k12, k2tog (14 sts).

Rows 66–74: Work in stockinette stitch, starting with a purl row.

Row 75: K2tog, knit to last 2 sts, k2tog (12 sts).

Rows 76–85: Repeat rows 66–75 (10 sts).

Rows 86–92: Work in stockinette stitch, starting with a purl row.

Row 93: Repeat row 75 (8 sts).

Rows 94–101: Repeat rows 86–93 (6 sts).

Rows 102–106: Work in stockinette stitch, starting with a purl row.

Row 107: Repeat row 75 (4 sts).

Rows 108–112: Work in stockinette stitch, starting with a purl row. Bind off knitwise.

Make a second side panel in the same way.

Zipper panels

Using size 8 (5 mm) needles, cast on (11 sts).
Row 1: (RS) Knit.
Row 2: K3, p8.
Rows 3–110: Repeat rows 1–2 another fifty-four times.
Bind off knitwise.
Make a second zipper panel in the same way.

Handles

Using size 6 (4 mm) needles, cast on 15 sts.
Starting with a knit row, work in stockinette stitch for 60 rows.
Bind off knitwise.

Inserting a zipper

Inserting a zipper can sometimes feel like a tricky process, but if you take your time and do not stretch the fabric, it is actually simple to do. Different zipper weights are suited to different types of yarn, so an Aran-weight yarn would need a medium to heavy zipper.

1 With the right side of the knitted fabric facing you, carefully pin the zipper into position so that the edges of the knitted fabric cover the zipper teeth. Baste it in place with a running stitch using a sharp sewing needle and thread. Remove the pins.

2 Sew the zipper in place using backstitch. If the yarn is too thick and bulky to sew in the zipper, try a thinner yarn in the same color, or use sewing thread. Use the knitting stitches and rows as a guideline to help to keep the zipper straight and even.

Finishing

With a tapestry needle, weave in the loose yarn tails to WS of work. Block and press the pieces to the required size (see schematic, right). Use the knitted pieces as templates to cut pieces of lining fabric. Lining the guitar case will prevent it from stretching too much under the weight of a guitar. Baste the lining pieces to the WS of the knitted pieces. Using mattress stitch, sew the long edges together on each handle. Attach one handle to the front panel, with one end over the shapings on rows 125–132 and the other end over the shapings on rows 103–110. Repeat for the back panel. Place back and front panels WS together and use mattress stitch to join the neck of the guitar case from marker to marker (row 133). Using a sewing needle and thread, backstitch the zipper to the ridged edges of the zipper panels (see step-by-step sequence on page 100). Join one short end of the zipper unit to the cast-on edge of a side panel. Repeat for the other end of the zipper unit. With WS together, pin the side panels and zipper into position from marker (row 133), around bottom, to marker (row 133) of back and front panels. Mattress stitch the side panels into place.

Schematic

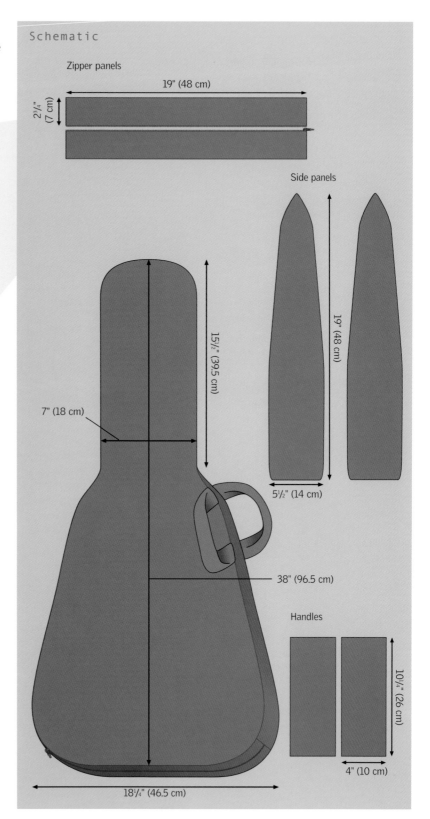

Zipper panels

19" (48 cm)

2¾" (7 cm)

Side panels

19" (48 cm)

5½" (14 cm)

15½" (39.5 cm)

7" (18 cm)

38" (96.5 cm)

Handles

10¼" (26 cm)

4" (10 cm)

18¼" (46.5 cm)

Record bag

This bag is great for carrying all your essentials around in. Knitted in stockinette stitch, the separate panels are then sewn together, making the seams a feature of the bag and adding to its structure and shape. The shoulder strap is worked in seed stitch, allowing it to lie flat. It looks fantastic embellished with the arty badges from pages 64–5.

THE KNITTY GRITTY

Size: 14" (35.5 cm)) wide x 14" (35.5 cm) high.
Yarn: Bulky-weight wool (100% wool; 109 yd [100 m] per 100 g ball): 4 balls.
Needles: Size 13 (9 mm); size 11 (8 mm). Adjust needle size if necessary to obtain correct gauge.
Notions: Tapestry needle.
Gauge: 11 sts x 14 rows = 4" (10 cm) in stockinette stitch using size 13 (9 mm) needles.

Abbreviations
k—knit
p—purl
RS—right side
st(s)—stitch(es)
WS—wrong side

Front and back

Using size 13 (9 mm) needles, cast on 40 sts.

Row 1: (RS) Knit.

Row 2: Purl.

These two rows form a stockinette stitch fabric. Continue to work in stockinette stitch for another 48 rows or until the work measures 14" (35.5 cm) from the cast-on edge, ending with a WS row. Bind off knitwise. Make a second panel for the back of the bag in the same way, this time binding off purlwise.

Side panels

Using size 13 (9 mm) needles, cast on 10 sts.

Beginning with a knit row, work in stockinette stitch for 50 rows or until the panel measures 14" (35.5 cm) from the cast-on edge, ending with a WS row. Bind off knitwise. Make two more side panels in the same way.

Handle

Using size 11 (8 mm) needles, cast on 9 sts.

Every row: K1, *p1, k1; repeat from * to end of row.

This row creates a seed stitch fabric. Continue in seed stitch until the handle measures about 43" (109 cm) or until the required length is achieved. Bind off in seed stitch.

Joining front and back

With a tapestry needle, weave in the loose yarn tails to the WS on all the pieces and press carefully. Using mattress stitch on the reverse stockinette stitch side of the fabric (that is, the purl side), sew the side panels to the front and back of the bag. This will create a cordlike seam on the outside of the bag. Turn the bag right side out.

Front flap

Using size 13 (9 mm) needles, with WS of back panel facing you, pick up 39 sts along the top of the back panel as follows: insert the needle under one loop (the loop facing you) of each bind-off stitch. The remaining loop of each bind-off stitch forms a ridge on the RS. If using single-point needles, work the pick-up from left to right so the needle point is in position to begin the next row. If using circular needles, pick up from either direction and slide the stitches into position to work the next row.

Row 1: (WS) Join yarn at beginning of row. K1, (p1, k1) twice, p29, k1, (p1, k1) twice.

Row 2: K1, (p1, k1) twice, p1, k27, p1, (k1, p1) twice, k1.

Repeat rows 1 and 2 another 15 times (32 rows total).

Next row: (RS) K1, *p1, k1: repeat from * to end.

Repeat last row eight times. Bind off in seed stitch.

Finishing

With a tapestry needle, weave in the loose yarn tails on the handle to the WS of work. With right sides together, whipstitch the handle into position at the open edges of the side panels.

musical pillow

This pillow features a guitar fretboard design and uses pretty shell buttons to indicate finger positions. Black and white yarns have been used here to produce a strikingly graphic pillow, but you could use any colors you wish. The button flap on the back of the pillow means that it's easy to remove the pillow form to wash the knitting if necessary.

THE KNITTY GRITTY

Size: About 12 x 12" (30.5 x 30.5 cm).

Yarn: DK-weight cotton (100% cotton; 93 yd [85 m] per 50 g ball): black (yarn A), 2 balls; cream (yarn B), 2 balls. Light-weight cotton (100% cotton; 125 yd [115 m] per 50 g ball): black (yarn C), 1 ball.

Needles: Size 3 (3.25 mm); size 5 (3.75 mm). Adjust needle size if necessary to obtain correct gauge.

Notions: Tapestry needle; seven ⅝" (15 mm) shell buttons for back fastening plus five extra buttons for finger positions; matching sewing thread and needle to sew on buttons; 12 x 12" (30.5 x 30.5 cm) pillow form.

Gauge: 17 sts x 26 rows = 4" (10 cm) in stockinette stitch using size 5 (3.75mm) needles and DK-weight yarn.

Abbreviations
k—knit
p—purl
RS—right side
st(s)—stitch(es)

Front panel
Using size 3 (3.25 mm) needles and yarn A, cast on 60 sts.
Rows 1–4: Starting with a knit row, work four rows in stockinette stitch.
Rows 5–20: Change to size 5 (3.75 mm) needles and work 16 rows in stockinette stitch. Continue in stockinette stitch, working the stripe sequence as indicated.
Rows 21–23: Yarn B.
Rows 24–25: Yarn A.
Rows 26–31: Yarn B.
Rows 32–33: Yarn A.
Rows 34–39: Yarn B.
Rows 40–41: Yarn A.
Rows 42–47: Yarn B.
Rows 48–49: Yarn A.
Rows 50–55: Yarn B.
Rows 56–57: Yarn A.
Rows 58–60: Yarn B.
Rows 61–76: Yarn A.
Rows 77–80: Change to size 3 (3.25 mm) needles and work the next four rows in yarn A. Bind off knitwise.

Back panel

Row 1: With right side facing, and using size 3 (3.25 mm) needles and yarn A, pick up and knit 60 sts from the cast-on edge of the front panel.

Row 2: Knit, then break off yarn A.

Row 3: Join yarn B and knit.

Row 4: Purl.

Rows 5–76: Change to size 5 (3.75 mm) needles and continue in stockinette stitch, starting with a knit row.

Rows 77–80: Change to size 3 (3.25 mm) needles and work four more rows in stockinette stitch.

Bind off knitwise.

Flap

Row 1: With right side facing, and using size 3 (3.25 mm) needles and yarn A, pick up and knit 60 sts from the bind-off edge of the pillow front.

Rows 2–3: Knit.

Row 4: K3, purl to last 3 sts, k3.

Rows 3–4 form the pattern repeat.

Rows 5–38: Change to size 5 (3.75 mm) needles and repeat rows 3–4 seventeen times (34 rows).

Change to size 3 (3.25 mm) needles.

Rows 39–40: Knit.

Row 41 (buttonhole row): K2, *bind off next 2 sts, knit until there are 7 sts on right needle counting from previous bind off; repeat from * until 4 sts remain, bind off 2 sts, knit to end (7 buttonhole spaces).

Row 42: Knit, casting on 2 sts over each buttonhole.

Rows 42–44: Knit.

Bind off purlwise.

Cut yarn, leaving a 4" (10 cm) tail.

Finishing

With a tapestry needle, weave in the loose yarn tails to WS of work. Fold the back panel right sides together onto the front panel and sew the side seams using backstitch. Turn right side out, then with a sewing needle and matching thread, sew buttons along the back panel to correspond with the buttonholes on the flap. Using yarn C and starting on the inside of the pillow, sew the frets (the thin vertical lines) onto the front panel, taking the needle through to the front of the panel over the top of the cream stripes and to the inside of the panel behind the black stripes. Sew buttons onto some of the frets where they cross the cream stripes to mark the finger positions. Match the placement of the frets and finger positions in the photograph or create your own design. Insert a pillow form and fasten the buttons.

Purple-passion disco top

Get up, get down, get funky with this super halter-neck top. Worked in a soft bulky cotton in an eye-catching purple, the openwork fabric on the lower section allows you to flash other colors underneath, while the beaded sequins are randomly scattered across the top to echo the lace pattern below.

THE KNITTY GRITTY

Size: Small [medium, large] to fit 34 [36, 38]" (86 [91, 97] cm) bust.

Yarn: Bulky-weight cotton (100% cotton; approx. 63 yd [58 m] per 50 g ball): purple, 5 balls.

Needles: Size 10 (6 mm); size 11 (8 mm). Adjust needle size if necessary to obtain correct gauge.

Notions: Stitch holder; tapestry needle; fifteen 8 mm sequins; fifteen 3 mm glass beads; sewing needle and thread.

Gauge: 12 sts x 17 rows = 4" (10 cm) in stockinette stitch using size 11 (8 mm) needles.

Abbreviations
k—knit
kp (in lace pattern)—k1, p1 into "yo twice" of previous row; see also step-by-step sequence on page 69
p—purl
RS—right side
skpo—slip 1 stitch, knit 1 stitch, pass slip stitch over
st(s)—stitch(es)
tbl—through back of loop
tog—together
WS—wrong side
yo—yarnover

Back

Using size 10 (6 mm) needles, cast on 58 [62, 66] sts.

Row 1: (RS) K2, *p2, k2, repeat from * to end.

Row 2: P2, *k2, p2, repeat from * to end.

Rows 1–2 form the ribbing.

Rows 3–5: Repeat rows 1–2 once, then row 1 again.

For small size only:

Row 6: *P2tog, k2, p2, k2tog, p2, k2; repeat from * to last 10 sts, p2tog, k2, p2, k2tog, p2 (48 sts).

For medium and large sizes only:

Row 6: P2, *k2tog, p2, k2, p2tog, k2, p2; repeat from * to last 0 [4] sts, 0 [k2, p2] (52 [56] sts).

Change to size 11 (8 mm) needles.

All sizes:

Row 7: (RS) *K2tog, yo twice, k2tog; repeat from * to end.

Row 8: *P1, kp, p1; repeat from * to end.

Row 9: Knit.

Row 10: Purl.

Row 11: K2, *skpo, yo twice, skpo; repeat from * to last 2 sts, k2.

Row 12: P2, *p1, kp, p1; repeat from * to last 2 sts, p2.

Row 13: Knit.
Row 14: Purl.
Rows 7–14 form the lace pattern.
Repeat rows 7–14 until back measures
12" (30.5 cm), ending with a WS row.**
Next row: Knit.
Next row: Purl.
Bind off knitwise.

Front

Work as instructed for the back until **.
Starting with a knit row, work six rows
in stockinette stitch.
Shape the top as follows.
Row 1: K2, skpo, knit to last 4 sts, k2tog,
k2 (46 [50, 54] sts).
Row 2: P2, p2tog, purl to last 4 sts,
p2tog tbl, p2 (44 [48, 52] sts).

Rows 3–4 [6, 6]: Repeat rows 1–2 once
[twice, twice] (40 [40, 44] sts).
Row 5 [7, 7]: Repeat row 1 (38 [38,
42] sts).
Row 6 [8, 8]: Purl.
Repeat the last two rows until 26 [28,
30] sts remain on needle.
Work two rows in stockinette stitch,
starting with a knit row.
Next row: Repeat row 1 (24 [26, 28] sts).
Work three rows in stockinette stitch,
starting with a purl row.
Work last four rows again (22 [24, 26] sts).

Neck

Row 1: (RS) K2tog, knit until 4 sts on
right needle, bind off 12 [14, 16] sts, knit
to last 5 sts, k3, k2tog.
Work each side of the neck separately.
Row 2: P2, p2tog tbl.

Row 3: Skpo, k1.
Row 4: P2tog. Fasten off.
With WS facing, rejoin yarn at neck edge.
Row 1: P2tog, p2.
Row 2: K1, k2tog.
Row 3: P2tog. Fasten off.

Joining the pieces

With a tapestry needle, weave in the loose
yarn tails to WS of work. Block and press
the pieces to the correct size. Sew the side
seams using backstitch or mattress stitch.

Neckband

With RS facing and using size 10 (6 mm)
needles, pick up and knit 3 sts down left
side of neck, 11 [13, 15] sts along front
neck, then 3 sts up right side of neck
(17 [19, 21] sts).
Bind off knitwise.

Left armhole border

With RS facing and using size 10 (6 mm)
needles, pick up and knit 30 [30, 32] sts
up left armhole, then cast on 80 sts for
the neck strap. Bind off knitwise.

Right armhole border

With RS facing and using size 10 (6 mm)
needles, cast on 80 sts for the neck strap,
then pick up and knit 30 [30, 32] sts
down right armhole. Bind off knitwise.

Finishing

With a sewing needle and thread, sew
sequins with glass beads on top onto the
stockinette section of the front piece,
arranging them symmetrically or randomly
(see page 65).

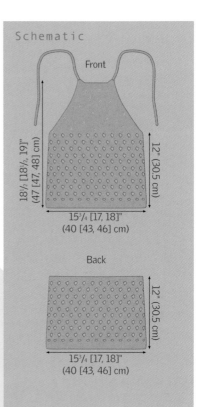

Schematic

Front

18½ [18½, 19]"
(47 [47, 48] cm)

12" (30.5 cm)

15¾ [17, 18]"
(40 [43, 46] cm)

Back

12" (30.5 cm)

15¾ [17, 18]"
(40 [43, 46] cm)

chapter 6

FESTIVAL FOLK

This chapter is full of wonderfully warm and fabulously functional festival wear. Keep cozy in the pixie hat and poncho, and let the two-tone socks take care of your toes. When you've finished using the picnic blanket during the day for your al fresco treats, you can wrap yourself in it during the cool evenings. For the ultimate in accessories, be the talk of the festival with a sporran bag —a kilt is optional!

Traditional sporran and shoulder bag

This quirky little project was inspired by the traditional Scottish Highland dress sporran. It is fun to make and looks fantastic. The main bag is worked in a bulky tweed yarn teamed with softer merino wool for the loopy texture at the front. Strap the bag around your hips or fling it across your shoulders—perfect for hands-free fun for both boys and girls.

THE KNITTY GRITTY

Size: About 6" (15 cm) wide x 6" (15 cm) high x 1" (2.5 cm) deep

Yarn: Bulky-weight tweed wool (100% pure new wool; 109 yd [100 m] per 100 g ball): blue or rust (yarn A), 2 balls per sporran. Bulky-weight wool (100% wool; 109 yd [100 m] per 100 g ball): blue or brown (yarn B), 1 ball per sporran.

Needles: Size 8 (5 mm); size 9 (5.5 mm).

Notions: Tapestry needle; 2½" (6.5 cm) wide buckle for traditional sporran; 1" (2.5 cm) button for each sporran.

Gauge: 15 sts x 20 rows = 4" (10 cm) in stockinette stitch using size 9 (5.5 mm) needles. Exact gauge isn't necessary.

Abbreviations

k—knit
m1—make 1 stitch by picking up horizontal bar before next stitch, putting it onto left needle, then knitting or purling into back of it as instructed
ML—make loop; see step-by-step sequence on page 111
p—purl
psso—pass slip stitch over
RS—right side
sl 1—slip 1
tbl—through back of loop
tog—together
WS—wrong side

Traditional sporran back

Using size 9 (5.5 mm) needles and yarn A, cast on 15 sts.
Row 1: (RS) Knit.
Row 2: Purl.
Row 3: K1, m1 knitwise, k13, m1 knitwise, k1 (17 sts).
Row 4: Purl.
Row 5: K1, m1 knitwise, k15, m1 knitwise, k1 (19 sts).
Row 6: Purl.
Row 7: K1, m1 knitwise, k17, m1 knitwise, k1 (21 sts).
Row 8: Purl.
Row 9: K1, m1 knitwise, k19, m1 knitwise, k1 (23 sts).
Rows 10–32: Work in stockinette stitch, starting with a purl row.
Row 33: K1, k2tog, k17, k2tog tbl, k1 (21 sts).
Row 34: Purl.
Row 35: K1, k2tog, k15, k2tog tbl, k1 (19 sts).
Row 36: Purl.
Bind off knitwise.

Front

Using size 9 (5.5 mm) needles and yarn B, cast on 15 sts.

Row 1: (WS) Knit.

Row 2: (RS) Knit.

Row 3: K1, m1 knitwise, *ML, k1, repeat from * to last 2 sts, ML, m1 knitwise, k1 (17 sts).

Row 4: Knit.

Rows 5–10: Repeat rows 3–4 three times (23 sts).

Row 11: *K1, ML, repeat from * to last stitch, k1.

Row 12: Knit.

Rows 13–32: Repeat rows 11–12 ten times.

Break off yarn B and join yarn A.

Row 33: Purl.

Row 34: K1, k2tog, k17, k2tog tbl, k1 (21 sts).

Row 35: Purl.

Row 36: K1, k2tog, k15, k2tog tbl, k1 (19 sts).

Row 37: Purl.

Bind off purlwise.

Flap

With RS of sporran back facing, and using size 9 (5.5 mm) needles and yarn A, pick up and knit

Loop stitch (ML—make loop)

This loopy knit stitch produces a shaggy surface where the knitted stitch is not really visible beneath the loops of yarn. The final effect depends on the yarn used, so the bulky soft merino yarn used here is ideal for a sporran. The finished loops can also be cut to give an alternative shaggy fur effect.

1 To make a loop, insert the right needle into the next stitch as if you were about to knit it. *Take the yarn around the right needle as if to knit and then wrap it around two fingers counter-clockwise, repeat from *, and then take the yarn around the needle again.

2 Pull all three loops through the stitch on the left needle, then place them on the left needle, leaving the original stitch on the left needle as well.

3 Knit all four loops together through the back of the loops.

19 sts along top straight cast-on edge.

Rows 1–2: Knit.

Row 3: (WS) P1, m1 purlwise, p17, m1 purlwise, p1 (21 sts).

Row 4: (RS) K1, m1 knitwise, k19, m1 knitwise, k1 (23 sts).

Rows 5–13: Work in stockinette stitch, starting with a purl row.

Row 14: K1, k2tog, k17, k2tog tbl, k1 (21 sts).

Row 15: Purl.

Row 16: K1, k2tog, k15, k2tog tbl, k1 (19 sts).

Row 17: P1, p2tog tbl, p13, p2tog, p1 (17 sts).

Row 18: K1, k2tog, k11, k2tog tbl, k1 (15 sts).

Row 19: P1, p2tog tbl, p9, p2tog, p1 (13 sts).

Row 20 (buttonhole row 1): K1, k2tog, k2, bind off 3 sts knitwise, (1 stitch on right needle), knit the next stitch, k2tog tbl, k1.

Row 21 (buttonhole row 2): P1, p2tog tbl, p1, cast on 3 sts, p1, p2tog, p1 (9 sts).

Row 22: K1, k2tog, k3, k2tog tbl, k1 (7 sts).

Row 23: P1, p2tog tbl, p1, p2tog, p1 (5 sts).
Bind off purlwise.

Belt

Using size 8 (5 mm) needles and yarn A, cast on 9 sts. Work in seed stitch (every row: *k1, p1, repeat from * to last st, k1) until work measures 18" (46 cm). Bind off in seed stitch. Make a second piece in the same way but measuring 28" (70 cm). Do not bind off. Shape the point of the belt as follows.

Row 1: P2tog, k1, p1, k1, p1, k1, p2tog (7 sts).

Row 2: K2tog, p1, k1, p1, k2tog (5 sts).

Row 3: P2tog, k1, p2tog (3 sts).

Row 4: Sl 1, k2tog, psso. Fasten off last stitch.

If you wish to lengthen or shorten the belt, simply adjust the number of rows of seed stitch you work.

Gusset

Using size 9 (5.5 mm) needles and yarn A, cast on 6 sts. Starting with a knit row, work in stockinette stitch until gusset measures 20" (51 cm), ending with a WS row. Bind off purlwise.

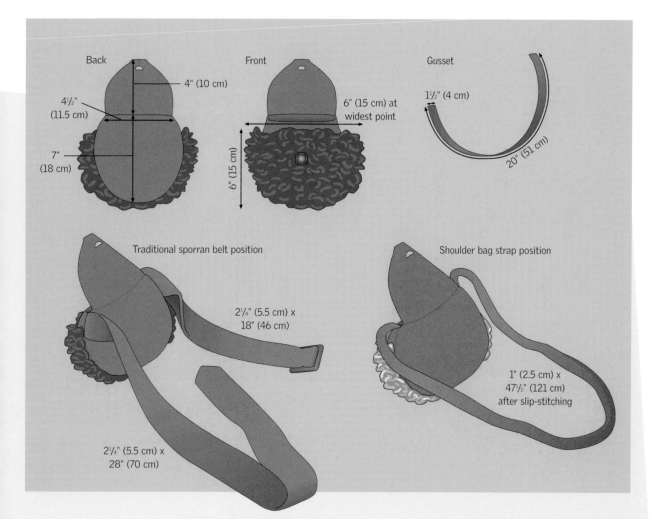

Back

4" (10 cm)

4½" (11.5 cm)

7" (18 cm)

Front

6" (15 cm) at widest point

6" (15 cm)

Gusset

1½" (4 cm)

20" (51 cm)

Traditional sporran belt position

2¼" (5.5 cm) x 18" (46 cm)

2¼" (5.5 cm) x 28" (70 cm)

Shoulder bag strap position

1" (2.5 cm) x 47½" (121 cm) after slip-stitching

Finishing

With a tapestry needle, weave in the loose yarn tails to WS of work. Press the back, flap, and gusset pieces. Do not press the front or belt. Sew the gusset and front pieces together using backstitch or mattress stitch. Sew the belt to the top side edges of the back piece in the same way, then sew the gusset to the back piece, stitching through all thicknesses where the belt is positioned. Sew the buckle to the end of the straight-edged belt strap. Sew a button onto the sporran front to correspond with the buttonhole on the flap.

Sporran shoulder bag

Make the shoulder bag in the same way as the traditional sporran, but make a shoulder strap instead of a belt as follows. Using size 8 (5 mm) needles and yarn A, cast on 7 sts.
Work in seed stitch (every row: *k1, p1, repeat from * to last st, k1) until shoulder strap measures 47½" (121 cm).
Bind off in seed stitch.

Finishing

Join the bag pieces together in the same way as the traditional sporran, but without the belt. Fold the strap in half lengthwise and slip-stitch the long edges together. Position the ends of the strap 1" (2.5 cm) from the top edges of the gusset piece on the inside of the bag and sew in place. Sew the button in place on the front, opposite the buttonhole in the flap.

flower-power poncho

Individualize your outfit with this 1960s-inspired poncho. The simple flowers are knitted in brightly colored cotton and sit delicately on the cozy eyelet trellis poncho. Have fun with different color combinations to create a retro poncho that will brighten anyone's day.

THE KNITTY GRITTY

Size: Approx. 30" (76 cm) long from base of neckband to lowest point at front; approx. 46" (117 cm) wide, measured across from seam to seam at widest point.

Yarn: Super bulky-weight wool (100% merino wool; 87 yd [80 m] per 100 g ball): blue (yarn A), 9 balls; DK-weight cotton (100% cotton; 93 yd [85 m] per 50 g ball): pink (yarn B), 2 balls; orange (yarn C), 1 ball.

Needles: For poncho—Size 17 (12 mm) straight needles; size 15 (10 mm) circular, 16" (40 cm). For flowers—Size 3 (3.25 mm). Adjust needle size if necessary to obtain correct gauge.

Notions: Stitch holder; tapestry needle; cardboard; crochet hook.

Gauge: 8 sts x 12 rows = 4" (10 cm) in stockinette stitch using size 17 (12 mm) needles.

Abbreviations
k—knit
p—purl
RS—right side
skpo—slip 1 stitch, knit 1 stitch, pass slip stitch over
st(s)—stitch(es)
tog—together
WS—wrong side
yo—yarnover

Back

Using size 17 (12 mm) needles, cast on 117 sts. Mark the center stitch.

Row 1: (RS) Knit to 2 sts before marked st, skpo, k1 (marked st), k2tog, knit to end (115 sts).

Row 2: Knit.

Row 3: K4, (k2tog, yo, k2) twelve times, k2tog, yo, k1, skpo, k1 (marked st), k2tog, k1, (k2tog, yo, k2) twelve times, k2tog, yo, k4 (113 sts).

Row 4: Purl.

Row 5: Knit to 2 sts before marked st, skpo, k1 (marked st), k2tog, knit to end (111 sts).

Row 6: Purl.

Row 7: K2, (k2tog, yo, k2) twelve times, k2tog, yo, k1, skpo, k1 (marked st), k2tog, k1, (k2tog, yo, k2) thirteen times (109 sts).

Row 8: Purl.

Row 9: Repeat row 5 (107 sts).

Row 10: Purl.

Row 11: K2tog, k2, (k2tog, yo, k2) eleven times, k2tog, yo, k1, skpo, k1 (marked st), k2tog, k1, (k2tog, yo, k2) twelve times, k2tog (103 sts).

Row 12: Purl.

Row 13: Repeat row 5 (101 sts).

Row 14: Purl.

Row 15: K1, (k2tog, yo, k2) eleven times, k2tog, yo, k1, skpo, k1 (marked st), k2tog, k1, (k2tog, yo, k2) eleven times, k2tog, yo, k1 (99 sts).

Row 16: Purl.

Row 17: Repeat row 5 (97 sts).

Row 18: Purl.

Row 19: K3, (k2tog, yo, k2) ten times, k2tog, yo, k1, skpo, k1 (marked st), k2tog, k1, (k2tog, yo, k2) ten times, k2tog, yo, k3 (95 sts).

Row 20: Purl.

Row 21: Repeat row 5 (93 sts).

Row 22: Purl.

Row 23: K2tog, k3, (k2tog, yo, k2) nine times, k2tog, yo, k1, skpo, k1 (marked st), k2tog, k1, (k2tog, yo, k2) nine times, k2tog, yo, k3, k2tog (89 sts).

Row 24: Purl.

Row 25: Repeat row 5 (87 sts).

Row 26: Purl.

Row 27: K2, (k2tog, yo, k2) nine times, k2tog, yo, k1, skpo, k1 (marked st), k2tog, k1, (k2tog, yo, k2) ten times (85 sts).

Row 28: Purl.

Row 29: Repeat row 5 (83 sts).

Row 30: Purl.

Row 31: Repeat row 5 (81 sts).

Row 32: Purl.

Row 33: K2tog, k2, (k2tog, yo, k6) four times, k2, skpo, k1 (marked st), k2tog, k4, (k2tog, yo, k6) four times, k2tog (77 sts).

Row 34: Purl.

Row 35: Repeat row 5 (75 sts).

Row 36: Purl.

Row 37: Repeat row 5 (73 sts).

Row 38: Purl.

Row 39: K7, (k2tog, yo, k6) three times, k2tog, yo, k1, skpo, k1 (marked st), k2tog, k5, (k2tog, yo, k6) three times, k2tog, yo, k3 (71 sts).

Row 40: Purl.

Row 41: K2tog, k31, skpo, k1 (marked st), k2tog, k31, k2tog (67 sts).

Row 42: Purl.

Row 43: Repeat row 5 (65 sts).

Row 44: Purl.

Row 45: K2, (k2tog, yo, k6) three times, k2tog, yo, k2, skpo, k1 (marked st), k2tog, k6, (k2tog, yo, k6) three times (63 sts).

Row 46: Purl.

Row 47: K2tog, k27, skpo, k1 (marked st), k2tog, k27, k2tog (59 sts).

Row 48: Purl.

Row 49: Repeat row 5 (57 sts).

Row 50: Purl.

Row 51: K2tog, k3, (k2tog, yo, k6) twice, k2tog, yo, k3, skpo, k1 (marked st), k2tog, k7, (k2tog, yo, k6) twice, k1, k2tog (53 sts).

Row 52: Purl.

Row 53: Repeat row 5 (51 sts).

Row 54: Purl.

Row 55: K2tog, k21, skpo, k1 (marked st), k2tog, k21, k2tog (47 sts).

Row 56: Purl.

Row 57: K7, k2tog, yo, k6, k2tog, yo, k4, skpo, k1 (marked st), k2tog, (k2tog, yo, k6) twice, k2tog, yo, k3 (45 sts).

Row 58: Purl.

Row 59: K2tog, k18, skpo, k1 (marked st), k2tog, k18, k2tog (41 sts).

Row 60: Purl.

Row 61: K2tog, k16, skpo, k1 (marked st), k2tog, k16, k2tog (37 sts).

Row 62: Purl.

Row 63: K2tog, k7, k2tog, yo, k5, skpo, k1 (marked st), k2tog, k1, k2tog, yo, k6, k2tog, yo, k3, k2tog (33 sts).

Row 64: Purl.

Row 65: K2tog, k12, skpo, k1 (marked st), k2tog, k12, k2tog (29 sts).

Row 66: Purl.

Row 67: K2tog, k10, skpo, k1 (marked st), k2tog, k10, k2tog (25 sts).

Row 68: Purl.

Row 69: Bind off 3 sts, knit to 2 sts before marked st, skpo, k1 (marked st), k2tog, knit to end (20 sts).

Row 70: Bind off 3 sts, purl to end (17 sts).

Row 71: Bind off 3 sts, knit to 2 sts before marked st, skpo, k1 (marked st), k2tog, knit to end (12 sts).

Row 72: Bind off 3 sts, purl to end (9 sts).

Slip the remaining 9 sts onto a stitch holder.

Front

Using size 17 (12 mm) needles, cast on 117 stitches. Mark the center stitch.

Rows 1–62: Work as for back (37 sts).

Row 63: (RS) K2tog, k7, k2tog, yo, k3, turn (13 sts).

Row 64: P2tog, purl to end (12 sts).

Row 65: K2tog, knit to last 2 sts, k2tog (10 sts).

Row 66: P2tog, purl to end (9 sts).

Row 67: K2tog, knit to last 2 sts, k2tog (7 sts).

Row 68: Purl.

Row 69: Bind off 3 sts, knit to end (4 sts).

Row 70: Purl.

Row 71: Bind off remaining 4 sts.

With RS facing, rejoin yarn to remaining 23 sts at neck edge.

Row 63: (RS) K2, skpo, k1 (marked st), k2tog, k9, k2tog, yo, k3, k2tog (20 sts).

Row 64: P11, p2tog, turn, slip remaining 7 sts onto a stitch holder (12 sts).

Row 65: K2tog, knit to last 2 sts, k2tog (10 sts).

Row 66: P2tog, purl to end (9 sts).

Row 67: K2tog, knit to last 2 sts, k2tog (7 sts).

Row 68: Purl.

Row 69: Knit.

Row 70: Bind off 3 sts, purl to end (4 sts).

Row 71: Knit.

Row 72: Bind off remaining 4 sts.

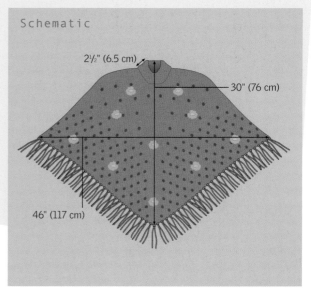

Fringe

Fringe is very easy to make. Cut a piece of cardboard ½" (1.2 cm) longer than the length of fringe you want to make. The cardboard should be wide enough to wrap the yarn around it as many times as required for the number of separate lengths of yarn you need, or use a narrower piece of cardboard and make the fringe in batches.

1 Wind the yarn around the cardboard length as many times as required. Cut through all the strands of yarn along one edge of the cardboard.

2 With the right side of the knitted fabric facing you, insert a crochet hook from wrong side to right side at the position of the first fringe. Fold two strands of yarn in half, catch the loop with the hook, and pull it through the knitting.

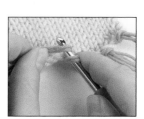

3 Catch the free ends with the hook and pull them through the loop. Pull the free ends to tighten the knot. Repeat as required.

Sewing up

With a tapestry needle, weave in the loose yarn tails on the poncho pieces to WS of work, then block and press. Sew the side seams with mattress stitch or backstitch.

Neck band

With a size 15 (10 mm) circular needle and RS facing, pick up and knit 8 sts down left front neck, 7 sts from back piece stitch holder, 8 sts up right front neck, and 9 sts from front piece stitch holder (32 sts).
Rounds 1–8: (K2, p2) to end.
Bind off loosely in rib and weave in the loose yarn tails.

Flowers

Using size 3 (3.25 mm) needles and yarn A, cast on 93 sts.
Row 1: K1, *k2, lift first of these 2 sts over second st, repeat from * to end (47 sts).
Row 2: (P2tog) to last st, p1 (24 sts).

Change to yarn B.
Row 3: Knit.
Row 4: Purl.
Row 5: K1, (k2tog) to last st, k1 (13 sts).
Break off the yarn, leaving a tail long enough to sew the flower to the poncho. Thread the tail on tapestry needle and pull through the remaining 13 sts, pull together, and fasten.

Finishing

Make some 6" (15 cm) long fringe (see step-by-step sequence above right) to go around the hem of the poncho. Each fringe should be made of two lengths of yarn. Place a fringe knot in every other stitch around the poncho hem, starting at the front point. Sew flowers onto the front and back of the poncho; refer to the photographs as a guide or place them in a pattern of your own choosing.

Schematic

2½" (6.5 cm)

30" (76 cm)

46" (117 cm)

Two-tone socks

Whether you're doing an outdoor pursuit, dozing in bed, or simply lazing around at home, these socks keep your feet warm and toasty. They have been given a fun twist by the use of a contrasting color to emphasize the tops, toes, and heels.

THE KNITTY GRITTY

Size: To fit average-sized woman's feet. Foot length from back of heel to toe: 9½" (24 cm). Leg length from top of sock to top of heel: 12" (30.5 cm).
Yarn: DK-weight wool (100% pure new wool; 124 yd [113 m] per 50 g ball): aquamarine (yarn A), 2 balls; cream (yarn B), 1 ball.
Needles: Size 3 (3.25 mm) double-pointed needles (dpns) set of 4. Size 6 (4 mm) dpns, set of 4. Adjust needle size if necessary to obtain correct gauge.
Notions: Tapestry needle; stitch marker.
Gauge: 20 sts x 29 rounds = 4" (10 cm) in stockinette stitch using size 6 (4 mm) needles.

Abbreviations
k—knit
p—purl
RS—right side
skpo—slip 1 stitch, knit 1 stitch, pass slip stitch over
ssk—slip 2 stitches knitwise, one at time, from left to right needle. Insert left needle tip into front loops of both slipped stitches and knit them together from this position
st(s)—stitch(es)
tbl—through back of loop
tog—together
WS—wrong side

Top of sock

Using size 3 (3.25 mm) needles and yarn B, cast on 52 sts. Join work into circle, arranging stitches with 17 sts on each of the first two needles and 18 sts on the third needle.
Rounds 1–9: *K2, p2, repeat from * to end.
This forms the ribbing.
Round 10: Rib 50 sts, p2tog (51 sts).
Change to size 6 (4 mm) needles and yarn A.
Rounds 11–26: Knit.

Leg shaping

Round 27: K2tog, k to last 2 sts, ssk (49 sts).
Rounds 28–32: Knit.
Rounds 33–44: Repeat rounds 27–32 twice (45 sts).
Continue knitting each round without shaping until leg measures 12" (30.5 cm) from cast-on edge or until required length is achieved. Arrange sts so that needle 1 has 11, needle 2 has 22, and needle 3 has 12.

Heel flap

Next row: K11; slip last 12 sts from needle 3 onto the beginning end of needle 1 (these 23 sts are for the heel flap). Divide remaining 22 sts onto two needles, or slip them onto a waste yarn stitch holder, to work as instep sts later. Change to yarn B and work in rows using two needles.
With WS facing, work on 23 heel sts as follows.
Row 1: (WS) Sl 1, p22.
Row 2: (RS) Sl 1, k22.
Rows 3–21: Repeat rows 1–2 nine more times, then row 1 again.

Heel turn (begin short-row shaping)

Row 22: (RS) Sl 1, k12, ssk, k1, turn.
Row 23: Sl 1, p4, p2tog, p1, turn.
Row 24: Sl 1, k5, ssk, k1, turn.
Row 25: Sl 1, p6, p2tog, p1, turn.
Row 26: Sl 1, k7, ssk, k1, turn.
Row 27: Sl 1, p8, p2tog, p1, turn.
Row 28: Sl 1, k9, ssk, k1, turn.
Row 29: Sl 1, p10, p2tog, p1, turn.
Row 30: Sl 1, k11, ssk, turn.
Row 31: Sl 1, p11, p2tog, turn (13 sts on needle).
Row 32: K7; place a stitch marker before the next stitch to denote the beginning of next round. This completes the heel, leaving 6 sts temporarily unworked on the left needle.

Heel gusset shaping

Slip the 22 instep sts onto one needle.
Change to yarn A. Using a spare needle and with RS facing, knit the 6 sts from left needle, then using the same needle, pick up and knit 15 sts along side of heel flap (21 sts). Using a second needle, knit across the 22 instep sts. Using a third needle, pick up and knit 14 sts along the other side of the heel flap, then k7 heel stitches (21 sts). (Total 64 sts).

Instep

Round 1: Knit.
Round 2: First needle: knit to last 3 sts, k2tog, k1; second needle: knit; third needle: k1, ssk, knit to end (62 sts). Repeat round 2 until 44 sts remain.

Foot

Work even, knitting every round, until foot length measures about 8" (20.5 cm) from back of heel.

Toe shaping

Change to yarn B.
Round 1: First needle: knit to last 3 sts, k2tog, k1; second needle: k1, ssk, knit to last 3 sts, k2tog, k1; third needle: k1, ssk, knit to end (40 sts).
Round 2: Knit.
Rounds 3–10: Repeat rounds 1–2 four more times (24 sts). Knit stitches from first needle onto end of third needle. With stitches divided equally on two needles, bind off sts using the 3-needle bind off (see step-by-step sequence below left).

Finishing

With a tapestry needle, weave in the loose yarn tails to WS of work.

Binding off two pieces together (3-needle bind off)

This is a way of joining two pieces of knitting together without having to sew them. The method creates a neat, firm seam when the two sets of stitches are bound off with right sides together and wrong sides facing the knitter, or can be made into a decorative feature when the stitches are bound off with wrong sides together and the right sides facing the knitter. The latter method is used here to join the top of the toes together, creating a seam on the outside of the socks because it would feel uncomfortable on the inside.

1 Place the two needles holding the stitches that are to be bound off in your left hand, with wrong sides together. Using a third needle in your right hand, insert the tip of this needle from front to back through the first stitch on both needles in your left hand. Knit these two stitches together, slipping them off the left needle once worked, leaving one stitch on the right needle.

2 Repeat this process with the next pair of stitches on the left needle so that you have two stitches on the right needle. Bind off the first stitch on the right needle in the usual way, by using one of the needles in your left hand to lift the first stitch on the right needle over the second stitch and off the end of the needle. Continue binding off in this way. When you reach the last pair of stitches, cut the yarn and thread it through both stitches. Pull tight to secure.

Pixie hat

This pointy pixie hat with cozy earflaps is knitted in a super bulky merino wool yarn. It is a great project for practicing your increasing and decreasing techniques, and can easily be made in an evening. The tonal blanket-stitch trim around the edges and extra-long ties frame the hat perfectly.

THE KNITTY GRITTY

Size: About 17" (43 cm) circumference at widest point. Fits average-sized adult head snugly.

Yarn: Super bulky-weight wool (100% merino wool; 87 yd [80 m] per 100 g ball): main color (yarn A), 1 ball. Extra super bulky-weight wool (100% merino wool; 33 yd [30 m] per 100 g ball): trim and ties (yarn B), 1 ball.

Needles: Size 15 (10 mm); size 17 (12 mm). Adjust needle size if necessary to obtain correct gauge.

Notions: Stitch holder; tapestry needle.

Gauge: 8 sts x 11 rows = 4" (10 cm) in stockinette stitch using size 17 (12 mm) needles.

Abbreviations
k—knit
m1—make 1 stitch by picking up horizontal bar before next stitch, putting it onto left needle, then knitting or purling into back of it as instructed
p—purl
psso—pass slip stitch over
RS—right side
skpo—slip 1 stitch, knit 1 stitch, pass slip stitch over
sl 1—slip 1 stitch
st(s)—stitch(es)
tog—together
WS—wrong side

Body of hat

The pattern starts at the pixie point of the hat.
Using size 17 (12 mm) needles and yarn A, cast on 4 sts.
Row 1: Purl.
Row 2: (RS) K1, (m1 knitwise, k1) three times (7 sts).
Row 3: Purl.
Row 4: Knit.
Row 5: P1, (m1 purlwise, p1) six times (13 sts).
Row 6: Knit.
Row 7: Purl.
Row 8: K1, (m1 knitwise, k2) six times (19 sts).
Row 9: Purl.
Row 10: Knit.
Row 11: (P3, m1 purlwise) six times, p1 (25 sts).
Row 12: Knit.
Row 13: Purl.
Row 14: (K4, m1 knitwise) six times, k1 (31 sts).
Row 15: Purl.
Row 16: Knit.
Row 17: Purl.
Row 18: (K5, m1 knitwise) six times, k1 (37 sts).
Rows 19–27: Work in stockinette stitch, starting with a purl row.
Change to size 15 (10 mm) needles.
Rows 28–33: Work in stockinette stitch, starting with a knit row.

Earflaps

Row 34: (RS) Bind off 4 sts knitwise, with 1 st already on right needle from bind-off, knit the next 8 sts, slip these 9 sts onto a stitch holder, bind off next 11 sts knitwise, with 1 st on right needle from bind-off, knit the next 8 sts (total of 9 sts), 4 sts remain, bind off 3 sts knitwise, cut yarn and thread through last stitch to fasten off—9 sts on needle, 9 sts on holder. With wrong side facing, rejoin yarn A to the 9 sts on the needle.
Row 35: Purl.
Row 36: Knit.
Row 37: Purl.
Row 38: K1, k2tog, k3, skpo, k1 (7 sts).
Rows 39–41: Work in stockinette stitch, starting with a purl row.
Row 42: K1, k2tog, k1 skpo, k1 (5 sts).
Row 43: Purl.
Row 44: K1, sl 1, k2tog, psso, k1 (3 sts).

Row 45: Purl.
Row 46: K3tog.
Fasten off the yarn, leaving a very long tail of at least 30" (76 cm).
With WS facing, slip the 9 sts from the stitch holder back onto the needle purlwise so the sts are untwisted, and rejoin yarn A. Repeat rows 35–46. Fasten off as before, leaving a very long tail of yarn.

Finishing

With a tapestry needle, weave in the loose yarn tails (but not the long ones at the earflaps) to WS of

work, then steam gently on WS. Sew the back seam using backstitch or mattress stitch.

Trim and ties

With a tapestry needle, join yarn B to the bottom of one earflap, leaving a long tail to match the one already there. Blanket stitch (see step-by-step sequence at right) around the edge of the earflap, across the back edge of the hat, and down to the bottom of the second earflap. Cut the yarn, leaving a long tail as before. Repeat along the front edges. Braid the three long tails of yarn at each earflap, finishing with a knot to secure the braid.

Blanket stitch

This is a great stitch for embellishing knitted edges. It also reinforces them and helps to stop them from curling.

1 Working from left to right, bring the threaded needle through the piece from the back to the front (right side) of the work, about one row in from the edge of the fabric.

2 Keeping the needle above the yarn, push the needle through to the back again, one stitch to the right. Point the needle upward, catch the loop of yarn around it, and pull the needle through.

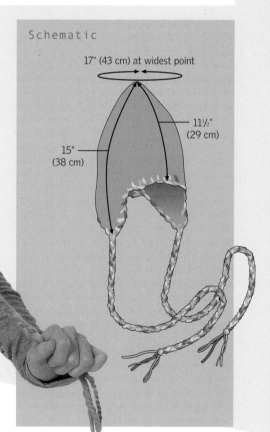

Schematic

17" (43 cm) at widest point

11½" (29 cm)

15" (38 cm)

Patchwork picnic blanket

This patchwork blanket is perfect for taking to a picnic. You can sit on it while the sun is shining, and wrap it around your shoulders when packing up at the end of the day if the weather cools. The bright multicolored stripes make a cheery statement that will put everyone in the mood for summer fun.

THE KNITTY GRITTY

Size: About 36 x 42"
(91 x 106 cm).
Yarn: DK-weight cotton
(100% cotton; 93 yd [85 m]
per 50 g ball): 1 ball each
of 12 different colors.
Sport-weight cotton
(100% cotton; 125 yd
[115 m] per 50 g ball): 1 ball
each of 12 different colors.
Needles: Size 3 (3.25 mm);
size 6 (4 mm); size 3
(3.25 mm) circular needle,
32" (80 cm) long. Adjust
needle size if necessary
to obtain correct gauge.
Notions: Tapestry needle.
Gauge: DK-weight squares:
20 sts x 28 rows = 4"
(10 cm) in stockinette stitch
using size 6 (4 mm) needles.
Sport-weight squares: 24 sts
x 34 rows = 4" (10 cm) in
stockinette stitch using
size 3 (3.25 mm) needles.

Abbreviations
RS—right side
st(s)—stitches

Note
This is a great project for
using up scraps of yarn, but
make sure they are all the
same weight. Although this
version is knitted in two
different weights to give a
textural patchwork effect,
you can keep it all the same
weight if you wish. Simply
follow the gauge guidelines
for the weight of yarn
you are using.

Knitting guide

DK-weight small-stripe squares	DK-weight large-stripe squares	Sport-weight small-stripe squares	Sport-weight large-stripe squares
A1 Green Orange Salmon pink **Make 3**	**B1** Green Salmon pink Orange **Make 3**	**C1** Red Hot pink Brown **Make 2**	**D1** Hot pink Red Brown **Make 3**
A2 Pink Brown Red **Make 2**	**B2** Pink Red Brown **Make 3**	**C2** Aqua Purple Magenta **Make 2**	**D2** Purple Aqua Magenta **Make 3**
A3 Soft green Blue Denim **Make 2**	**B3** Blue Soft green Denim **Make 3**	**C3** Blue Yellow Pale blue **Make 3**	**D3** Yellow Blue Pale blue **Make 3**
A4 Aqua Purple Lilac **Make 2**	**B4** Aqua Lilac Purple **Make 3**	**C4** Terra-cotta Orange Green **Make 2**	**D4** Orange Terra-cotta Green **Make 3**

A and B squares

Using size 6 (4 mm) needles and the first color listed in the relevant section of the above knitting guide, cast on 31 sts. Starting with a knit row, work 42 rows in stockinette stitch, alternating the colors every three rows for an A square and every six rows for a B square. Bind off knitwise.

C and D squares

Using size 3 (3.25 mm) needles and the first color listed in the relevant section of the above knitting guide, cast on 37 sts. Starting with a knit row, work 48 rows in stockinette stitch, alternating the colors every three rows for a C square and every six rows for a D square. Bind off knitwise.

Finishing

With a tapestry needle, weave in the loose yarn tails to WS of work on all 42 squares, then block and press them. Sew the squares together in columns of seven, using backstitch or mattress stitch, in the sequence set out in the finishing guide opposite. Start column 1 with the stripes of the first square horizontal, the second square vertical, and so on down the column. Start column 2 with the stripes of the first square vertical, the second square horizontal, and so on down the column. Continue alternating the orientation of the stripes on alternate squares and columns. Join all the columns together and press the seams.

Finishing guide

Column 1	Column 2	Column 3	Column 4	Column 5	Column 6
B1	D4	B4	D1	B3	D2
C3	A1	C4	A4	C1	A3
B2	D3	B1	D4	B4	D1
C2	A2	C3	A1	C4	A4
B3	D2	B2	D3	B1	D4
C1	A3	C2	A2	C3	A1
B4	D1	B3	D2	B2	D3

Edging

Use a different color yarn for each side of the blanket, or stripe the edging if you are using small scraps of yarn. With RS facing and using a size 3 (3.25 mm) circular needle and DK-weight yarn, pick up and knit 198 stitches along the top edge of the blanket.
Rows 1–5: Knit.
Bind off purlwise.
Repeat along the lower edge of the blanket.
Do the same along each side edge, but pick up and knit 220 stitches this time.
Weave in the loose yarn tails and press the seams.

Yarn directory

Below is a list of the specific yarns used to make the projects. If you cannot find any of these yarns or simply wish to make a project in a different yarn, use the information supplied at the beginning of each project, where you will find the quantity, weight, and fiber content of the yarns. Additional advice on substituting yarns can be found on page 12.

Urban Playground

Knee-pad covers
Yarn: Rowan Handknit Cotton; colors & codes: A = Double Choc 315, B = Seafarer 318.

Power wristbands
Yarn: Rowan Handknit Cotton; colors & codes: A = Seafarer 318, B = Double Choc 315.

Key chain
Yarn: Rowan Denim; color & code: Ecru 324.

iPod covers
Yarn: Rowan Handknit Cotton; colors & codes: 20GB iPod—A = Decadent 314 and B = Slick 313, or A = Gooseberry 219 and B = Celery 309; iPod mini—A = Diana 287 and B = Seafarer 318, or A = Sugar 303 and B = Slick 313, or A = Mango Fool 319 and B = Flame 254.

Striped beanie
Yarn: Rowan Wool Cotton; colors & codes: A = Deepest Olive 907, B = Tender 951.

Hooded top
Yarn: Rowan Plaid; colors & codes: A = Hearty 156, B = Bramble 157.

Textured zip-up top
Yarn: Rowan All Seasons Cotton; color & code: Jersey 191.

Night Owls

Distressed hole sweater
Yarn: Rowan Yorkshire Tweed Chunky; color & code: Olive Oil 557.

Extra-long skinny scarf
Yarns A & B: Rowan Cotton Glace; colors & codes: A = Hot Lips 818, B = Poppy 741. Yarn C: Rowan Lurex Shimmer; color & code: Bedazzled 338.

Fingerless gloves
Yarn: Rowan Wool Cotton; colors & codes: A = Elf 946, B = Antique 900.

Arty badges
Yarn A: Rowan Big Wool; color & code: Pip 015. Yarn B: Rowan Yorkshire Tweed DK; color & code: Frog 349. Yarn C: Rowan Yorkshire Tweed 4 ply; color & code: Lustre 282.

Party dress
Yarn A: Rowan Cotton Rope; color & code: Black 066. Yarn B: Rowan Cotton Glace; color & code: Black 727.

Baubles and bangles
Yarn: Rowan Big Wool; colors & codes: White Hot 001 (narrow basic bangle), Pip 015 (wide basic bangle), Ice Blue 021. Yarn: Rowan Biggy Print; colors & codes: Razzle Dazzle 246 (hole bangle), Splash 248. Yarn: Rowan Chunky Print; color & code: Shriek 081. (All the yarns are used for making the necklace beads.)

Home Comforts

Fruit protectors
Yarn: Rowan Handknit Cotton; colors & codes: apple—Rosso 215 and Gooseberry 219, banana—Buttercup 320 and Double choc 315.

Egg cozies
Yarn A: Rowan Kidsilk Haze; color & code: Candy Girl 606. Yarn B: Rowan 4 ply Soft; color & code: Wink 377.

Knitted washcloths
Chenille yarn: Rowan Chunky Cotton Chenille; color & code: Ecru 365. Cotton yarn: Rowan R2 Rag; color & code: Cream 002.

Cozy toe slippers
Yarn: Rowan Big Wool; color & code: Smoky 007.

Punk Garage Rocks

Safety-pin sweater
Yarn: Rowan Big Wool; colors & codes: A = Camouflage 023, B = Pistashio 029.

Guitar case
Yarn: Rowan All Seasons Cotton; color & code: Military 213.

Festival Folk

Traditional sporran and shoulder bag
Yarn A: Rowan Yorkshire Tweed Chunky; colors & codes: Pecan 553 (traditional), Coast 555 (shoulder bag). Yarn B: Rowan Chunky Print: colors & codes: Pit 080 (traditional), Deep End 076 (shoulder bag).

Flower-power poncho
Yarn A: Rowan Big Wool; color & code: Blue Velvet 26. Yarns B & C: Rowan Handknit Cotton; colors & codes: B = Slick 313, C = Mango Fool 319.

Snuggle blanket
Yarn: Rowan Plaid; color & code: Spicy 154.

Felted buttons
Yarn: Rowan Yorkshire Tweed DK; colors & codes: Goose 352, Scarlet 344.

Houndstooth dog coat
Yarn: Rowan Yorkshire Tweed DK; A = Scarlet 344, B = Skip 347.

Easy-care cacti
Beaded cactus yarn: Rowan Kid Classic; color & code: Battle 845. Seed stitch cactus yarn: Rowan Wool Cotton; color & code: Elf 946.

Record bag
Yarn: Rowan Chunky Print; color & code: Temper 073.

Musical pillow
Yarns A & B: Rowan Handknit Cotton; colors & codes: A = Black 252, B = Ecru 251. Yarn C: Rowan Cotton Glace; color & code: Black 727.

Purple-passion disco top
Yarn: Rowan Cotton Rope; color & code: Parma 063.

Two-tone socks
Yarn: Rowan Yorkshire Tweed DK; colors & codes: A = Skip 347, B = Goose 352.

Pixie hat
Yarn A: Rowan Big Wool; color & code: Pip 015. Yarn B: Rowan Biggy Print; color & code: Shock 247.

Patchwork picnic blanket
DK-weight yarn: Rowan Handknit Cotton in various colors. Sportweight yarn: Rowan Cotton Glace in various colors.

Index

Author acknowledgments

Many thanks to Kate Buller and the rest of the team at Rowan for their help and support, and for the use of the lovely Rowan yarns.

Thanks also to Kate Kirby and Michelle Pickering at Quarto for giving me the opportunity to create this book with my dear friend and fellow knitting fanatic Julie Marchington.

Thanks also to my Mum (Sandra Youngson) and Irene Jackson for helping us create the projects, and to all my friends and loved ones for putting up with me. A huge thanks to Steph and Stew Marchington, who were a great sounding board, helping us to keep everything fresh and funky! Thanks also to Will Marchington for the support he gave Julie and myself throughout the whole process.

I would like to dedicate this book to the memory of Julie Marchington, for her wicked sense of humor, inspiration, and passion. She was a fantastic lady who lived life to the fullest. Her untimely passing has saddened many.